Using the
Power of *Poetry*

to Teach Language Arts, Social Studies, Science, and More

By David L. Harrison and Kathy Holderith

Nov. 8, 2003

Dear Charlotte,

So wonderful to meet you.

May you find poetry everywhere!

Warmly

Kathy Holderith

SCHOLASTIC
PROFESSIONAL BOOKS

New York • Toronto • London • Auckland • Sydney
Mexico City • New Delhi • Hong Kong • Buenos Aires

Dedication

To my husband, Ric, for his insight, countless hours of
proofreading, and ever-present support.   —KH

To Kent Brown
for believing in poetry,
and in poets.   —DLH

Acknowledgments

A heartfelt thanks to Shelley Harwayne and Georgia Heard for the invaluable lessons they shared. To Sue
Lubeck, owner of The Bookies, for her ongoing encouragement. To Honey Goldberg for always being there.

To my family, my C.C.I.R.A. friends, and my colleagues, my principal, and friends, at Ben Franklin
Elementary School. To my students, past and present, whose ability to write never ceases to amaze me.

Lastly, to my friend, David Harrison, who helped me find my voice, and to our creative, insightful, and
sensitive editor, Joanna Davis-Swing, who shaped this book and made it a reality.

—KH

Writing a book with another person, especially when your partner lives in Colorado and you live in
Missouri, takes determination, planning, coordination, cooperation and, above all, shared visions. To Kathy
Holderith go my thanks and gratitude for being a totally supportive, enthusiastic friend and partner who has
taught me much about the classroom. I have also learned and benefited from the suggestions, examples, and
gentle nudges toward a better way that so many good teachers have contributed to this book.

— DLH

The authors and editors thank Boyds Mills Press for their permission to reprint several of
David's poems that have appeared previously in *Somebody Catch My Homework* (1992),
Wild Country (1999), and *The Alligator in the Closet* (2003).

Every effort has been made to find the authors and publishers of the
poems in this book and obtain permission to print them.

Cover design and illustration by Gemare Falzarano
Interior design by Sydney Wright
Interior photographs by Ric Holderith and Kathy Holderith
Interior illustrations by Amanda Harvey

ISBN 0-439-28232-2
Copyright © 2003 by David L. Harrison and Kathy Holderith
All rights reserved.
Printed in the U.S.A.
1 2 3 4 5 6 7 8 9 10   40   09 08 07 06 05 04 03

Contents

Poet's Note

As a little boy I loved many things. The outdoors. Camping with my parents. Exploring along the lakeshores. Climbing trees. The wildness and strangeness of creatures I met fascinated me. I watched them, listened to them, wondered about their lives. I was encouraged by my parents, teachers, and adult friends to draw pictures and make up poems inspired by the things I saw and wondered about.

Years later, I graduated with degrees in biology from Drury University and Emory University. At Drury, I also rediscovered the pleasure of writing. After a period of searching for the right genre, my life changed forever when I wrote a book for children, *The Boy With a Drum*. That experience, like a compass, set the course for all that was to follow.

Another important event of self-discovery occurred in 1993, when *Somebody Catch My Homework* was published. Writing that first book of poetry fulfilled an old promise to myself. Holding the book in my hands at last was one of those moments you don't forget. I felt like a climber on top of the peak. I was fifty-six.

I've been other things—husband, father, musician, scientist, editor, businessman—but through them all I've remained a writer. I start early each morning writing. Writers, I can tell you, are a dedicated lot.

Now it is my pleasure to join forces with Kathy Holderith, friend, master teacher, and lover of poetry. One of the beliefs we share is that poetry can bring new meaning and dimension to just about any subject or situation in the classroom throughout the year.

Though young people share our lives, they live most truly in a place where miracles seem not only possible but imminent. For them the time between swallowing the last bite and being excused from the table can seem an unbearable eternity. Astronomer Carl Sagan says, "We are like butterflies who flutter for a day and think it is forever." That is especially true of the state we call childhood, and poetry is a wonderful way to help students capture glimpses of their emerging truths like snapshots in an album of their future.

Teacher's Note

For as long as I can remember, books have always been an integral part of my life. As a young child, I listened to my mother read a wide variety of books to my sister and me. From *My Book House* she read stories and poems such as "The Little Red Hen," "Wynken, Blynken, and Nod," and "The Gingerbread Man." She shared many Golden Books, too. My favorite Golden Book was entitled *Let's Go Shopping*. The poems and stories were not read just once. They were shared over and over again. "Read it again, Mother! Read it again!" we would plead. My sister and I would pour over the words, the illustrations, the story line, the message . . . . My love affair with literature was just beginning.

The summer of 1971 found me traveling to Germany to visit a friend. As luck would have it, there was an opening in her school. I got the job and for the next two years I taught on an American army base for the Department of Defense in Babenhausen, Germany. While in Germany, I remember discussing with my colleagues how poetry could be incorporated into all subject areas. That notion stuck. From that time on, each year I found many ways to integrate poetry in my classroom.

Now fast-forward to February 1995: It was a cold evening and I was meeting a group of poets and authors for dinner. In walked David Harrison, a tall gentleman with a quiet smile. He was a featured poet and author at our Colorado State Reading Conference, and it was my privilege to be his hostess. I had read his award-winning poetry book *Somebody Catch My Homework* and had shared it with my class. They loved it! But at that time, I had no idea of the breadth of his talent and his enormous commitment to helping the children of Springfield, Missouri, in the literacy arena.

At a session during the reading conference, David spoke of his background in science, his endeavors with music, and his special Springfield projects in which he challenged many students to reach "sky high" to become better readers and writers. With his dry Missouri humor and his wide range of stories and poems, he totally captivated our audience.

In the past several years, David has taught me many valuable lessons. It is an honor and a privilege for me to collaborate on this book with David Harrison—person and poet extraordinaire.

Kathy Holderith

*I*ntroduction

*I*n our fast-paced, "instant everything" world, we need poetry. It helps children and adults to ponder, to observe, to ask questions, to discover sights, sounds, and feelings that otherwise might remain untapped. It brings balance and beauty to our increasingly complex world. Poetry can awaken our senses or bring the element of surprise into our lives. It makes us laugh, teaches us powerful lessons, and renews our souls.

Poetry fits perfectly into the classroom. Never mind how complicated and difficult we adults may try to make it. "In the beginner's mind there are many possibilities," says Shunryu Suzuki. "In the expert's mind there are few." Students just grab their pencils and get on with their work. It's our job to stand back and let them explore their possibilities by writing poems based on the world as they see it so far.

Writing poems about the subjects they are studying reinforces students' learning. Poetry challenges them to observe, to decide what they want to say and how they feel about what they know. Writing poems stimulates critical thinking by bringing important information into sharper focus. It's an excellent vehicle for learning, and we encourage teachers to experiment with poetry in the classroom. You'll be amazed by the results.

Teaching With Poetry

In school, poetry is a highly accessible and easily approachable genre for children. Students who read poems and share them aloud begin to feel comfortable writing them. They need to see strong adult- and student-made examples of poetry. We as teachers need to give them direction and guidance through the use of focus lessons, discovery lessons, and discussions. We can teach a great deal about the craft of writing with carefully planned poetry lessons.

We need to compose poetry in front of students. Shelley Harwayne says, "We need to share the roots of writing; not just the flowers." Donald Graves, in his book *Explore Poetry*, states, "Poetry, like music, involves an enormous range of individual taste." Children should be exposed to a wide range of poetry to be able to write different types of poetry and to decide which poems are most appealing to them.

Poetry should be celebrated and cultivated. It can be incorporated into every curricular area. Many of the multiple intelligences Howard Gardner

describes (see *Multiple Intelligences*, 1993) may be woven in. Musical instruments, background music, clapping, tapping, snapping, and art may be used to enhance poetry presentations. Poetry can provide a novel way to teach skills such as strong verbs and the element of surprise in the language arts arena. Research skills in social studies, math, science, and other subjects can be presented in a fresh way by embedding the knowledge within a carefully crafted poem. Interpretation is limited only by one's imagination. We've packed this book with ideas from our own experience and from teachers all over the country who share our passion for poetry. But we hope it's only the beginning; we hope you will take these ideas and run with them, developing your own ways of integrating poetry into your teaching.

How to Use This Book

Welcome to a year filled with poetry! We begin by presenting practical ideas and strategies that will help you introduce poetry in a fun way and sustain students' interest in reading and writing poetry all year.

We share units and mini units that we've used with success—Kathy as a third grade teacher in Colorado and David as a visiting poet in classrooms all over the world. The lessons, ideas, and examples come from our experience— especially Kathy's third grade classroom—but we trust you will adapt what we've done to suit the needs and interests of your particular students. Many of these lessons relate to a season or a particular curricular area. In addition to the following elements, some units include graphic organizers, checklists, rubrics, or other ready-to-use materials.

Unit components include

> ✳ focus lessons,
>
> ✳ suggested materials,
>
> ✳ introduction,
>
> ✳ example lessons,
>
> ✳ display and/or extension ideas, and
>
> ✳ model poems.

We do not want writers with laryngitis. We want poets who have voices that laugh, cry, question, and even shout. It is our dream that the lessons in this book will inspire your students to explore the world and express themselves through the power of poetry.

Because good literature is precise, intelligent, colorful, sensitive, and rich in meaning, it offers the child his best hope of expressing what he feels.
   –Jim Trelease

CHAPTER 1

25 Great Ideas For Your Classroom

> From you I receive,
>
> To you I give,
>
> Together we share,
>
> From this we live.
>
> —traditional Sufi song

Many friends contributed ideas to this collection. Like a good menu, its entrees are well tested by successful teachers and administrators who know how to excite students and get them involved in the learning process.

If one idea doesn't seem right for your teaching style (or the learning styles of your students), move on to another. A few of the techniques can become yearlong activities (see Ruth Nathan's "Friday Fishbowl," page 20, and Vicki Ogden's "Poetry Time," page 21). Some are meant to introduce a new tool or concept (such as Kathy's "Poetry Search," on the next page, and Merrillyn Kloefkorn's "Selecting a Topic," see page 20). You'll find great ways to introduce poetry into your classroom and put it to work as an exciting method to hook your students on writing as they learn.

The driving force of this book is our belief that poetry can be an effective teaching tool across the curricula throughout the year. We hope the ideas in this chapter inspire you to weave more poetry into your teaching.

1 In the Bag: Building Community

from Kathy

This is an excellent activity to present at the beginning of the year to help students learn about one another and develop a sense of community. I write a note inviting students to bring in items that will tell the class about a hobby or interest they have, a sport they play, or a place they visited. All the items must fit in a paper bag, so photographs of pets or vacation spots can be brought in.

I model taking items out of my own bag one by one and talking about each, sharing information about myself. I then hand out the notes and bags and ask everyone to be ready to share in a few days. On the designated day, I put students in groups of three or four and ask them to share the items in their bags. After each person finishes talking, the group members write two to three things they learned about their classmate in their notebook.

When the groups have finished sharing, I gather the class together and model writing a poem about one of the items from my bag. Then I ask students to write their own poem about one of their items, which they share in small groups of two to three.

2 Poetry Search: Discovering Poetry Anthologies

from Kathy

I gather my students in our reading area and introduce the focus lesson: *Poems are sometimes collected in books called anthologies. Anthologies can be organized by theme, by poet, or by time period.* I show the class examples of each type of poetry book.

Then I pass out a "Types of Poetry Books" recording sheet to each child (see sample at right) and announce that we are going on a "poetry search." Before the lesson, I have set up five stations (or groups of books) around the room, with six or more poetry books per station. I divide my class into groups of five, and describe the procedure for the search: "When I ring the bell, I would like each of you to go to your assigned station with your sheet, a clipboard, and a pencil. Once you are at your station, please work with your group. Skim and scan as many books as possible. Decide which categories the books fit into and record your findings on the sheet. Work fast! When I ring the bell again, I would like each group to rotate to the next station." Students are eager to begin and get right to work as soon as I ring the bell.

This is a quick way for the class to preview a large number of poetry books in a short amount of time. Students can choose to read any of these books during

Name _____ Date _____

An *anthology* is a collection of writing. Poems are often printed in anthologies. Poetry anthologies can be arranged by theme, by poet, or by time period, or they can be a general collection of poems. Sometimes single poems are published alone.

Use this sheet to categorize the kinds of poetry books you explore during this activity. Write the title of the book under the category to which it belongs.

Types of Poetry Books

1. Anthology arranged by theme
_____
_____

2. Anthology arranged by time period
_____
_____

3. Anthology of one poet's work
_____
_____

4. A single poem
_____
_____

5. General anthology of different types of poems
_____
_____

free reading time or during a poetry unit. I adapted the idea for the poetry search from my teaching partner, Ann Connell-Allen, who sometimes uses the book station method when she is introducing a new science or social studies unit to her students to familiarize them with the range of resources available on the topic.

③ Poetry Pack Rat: Sharing Poetry With Families

from Kathy

Dear Parents,

This year you are invited to participate in our "Poetry Pack Rat" project. The goal of the project is to help students develop a love of poetry by sharing beautiful poems with their families. Your child will bring home a book bag containing:

- a poetry book
- an Idea Sheet
- a journal

The journal is a place to record your family's favorite poem and to share the reasons <u>why</u> your family enjoyed it.

Poetry brings sound and sense together in words and lines, ordering them on the page in such a way that both the writer and reader get a different view of life.

Georgia Heard, author of <u>For the Good of the Earth and Sun</u>, states, "Every writer of poetry is first a reader of poetry." It is my hope that this project will not only encourage our students to become readers of poetry; it will encourage them to become writers of poetry.

Most sincerely,
Your child's teacher

Here's a great way to invite students and their families to read and discuss poetry at home. Place a poetry book, a journal, and an Idea Sheet (see page 11) in a canvas bag. Send the bag home with a student for two or three days. Encourage students and their parents to read the poems aloud together, talk about and reread them (using the Idea Sheet for inspiration), and record their thoughts in the journal.

Include a note like the one on the left to explain the idea of Poetry Pack Rat, and give families suggestions for reading and enjoying poetry together.

Note: I wrote a grant to cover the cost of the bags, books, and journals.

④ Poetry, Song, and Rap Folders: Collecting and Sharing Verse

from Kathy

At the beginning of every year, I ask each child to bring in a pocketed three-prong folder. Students label and decorate their folders and add poems, songs, and raps throughout the year. I encourage them to include a wide range of items in their folders: patriotic songs, humorous poems, poems that students have written, poems that have a beat that repeats, and poems that contain strong messages. Sometimes students take their folders home and share the pieces with their parents. Many of the poems are revisited during silent reading, and I also use the poems as writing models when we're discussing descriptive language, strong verbs, and other writing techniques.

from David

A couple of musician friends have put several of my poems to music. With a little help from a guitar, some rhythm, and voices willing to sing, many poems can take on new personality and dimension. It might be fun to see what your students can do with their favorite selections if you encourage them with a classroom rhythm section and maybe a little bit of coffeehouse atmosphere.

Idea Sheet

As you read and talk about poems with your child, you may want to try out some of these ideas that I've adapted from Georgia Heard, a renowned poet and inspired teacher.

> "Every writer of poetry is first a reader of poetry."
> —Georgia Heard, *For the Good of the Earth and Sun*

1. Keep a notebook to collect poems that you love. You might want to keep two collections: one for your child and one for yourself.

2. Read poems that will open the doors to feelings and imagination.

3. Here are a few tips when reading a poem aloud to your child:

- First, respect the mood of the poem—somber and slow, light and playful, reflective, or exhilarating.

- Read it slowly enough for your child to piece it together.

- Respect the white space; it means silence—a visual and aural pause. The way the lines are broken and the way the poem is arranged on the page is the code the poet uses to indicate how the poem should be read.

- Read a poem all the way through the first time.

- Read in as natural a voice as possible.

- Let your child see the poem that you've been reading, either by giving him or her a copy or by copying the poem in large type.

5 What I've Learned So Far: Discovering the Wisdom of Youth

from David

A few years ago, I asked students in the Springfield, Missouri, public school district to tell me what they had learned so far. More than 10,000 students (prekindergarten through grade 12), educators, and support staff contributed brief bits of learned wisdom. Several teacher-editors and I selected 1,100 quotations and published a book appropriately titled *What I've Learned So Far*. Students also illustrated the 160-page volume. I recommend the project if you have someone to lead the effort.

However, the process can be done on any scale that suits your needs. In one school I worked only with second-graders and asked them to tell me what they'd learned so far. Three days later we held an assembly and the students took turns reading what they had written to an audience of appreciative teachers, students, and parents.

This approach to writing encourages students to think and to write about their thoughts. Everyone can contribute, it doesn't take long, and it stands on its own as a writing exercise. But if you want to take the next step, ask your students to turn their brief pieces of prose into poems. They may work on their own or you may work with the class to create one or more collective poems.

from Kathy

I'd also suggest compiling a class book of these verses and/or display the verses in the hall during parent conferences. Parents will certainly be entertained!

6 Authors' Tea: Sharing Our Poetry and Writing

from Kathy

In schools everywhere, children write stories and their pieces are honored at "Authors' Teas." My partner, Ann Connell-Allen, and I have expanded the concept to ask each child to select one story and one poem that they would like to share. Students practice reading their stories and poems several times during class so they are prepared to do their best job at the tea. We invite all family members, including grandparents, to attend. We have a large, decorated chocolate cake and delicious punch. Everyone has a wonderful time. It is a memorable celebration, and the students truly feel that they are authors!

7 Read Poetry Aloud With Feeling: Getting Comfortable Before an Audience

from Kathy

I ask students to get out their Poetry, Song, and Rap Folders. We select a poem.

Everyone stands, reads the title, and sits down. Next I say, "If your birthday is in May, June, or July, stand up and read the first stanza. Read the stanza with feeling!" (Then they sit down.) After that, I might say, "If you have green eyes or blue eyes, stand up and read stanza two with lots of expression!"

It is also fun to have the students give you suggestions (for example, students who play soccer should stand, or people with red hair).

This is one way to keep them on their toes and actively involved!

from David

Sometimes I talk about how important it is to read poetry with feeling. I kid students about working hard to write about how they feel and then mumbling when they read their poems aloud. I tell them that poems used to be sung or acted on a stage. In my own case, I can sing (sort of!) some of my own poems that have been set to music. You can take a song that your students recognize and read the lyric aloud as a poem, then sing the song to underscore the connection between the poem and its music.

Next, I tell students that we're going to practice reading their work aloud. I take one or two short poems (not theirs) and read them two ways: first I mumble them without expression; then I read them dramatically. We share the laugh. Then I ask for my first "victim" or my first "guinea pig." Usually, someone seems eager to read his poem. I invite the student to sit beside me, face the class, introduce himself, give the name of his poem, and read to us. I keep the mood light by teasing, "We've never seen you before, sir, so you'll have to tell us who you are."

After the reading, we clap. We always applaud. That's the rule.

Then I say something like, "That was wonderful! Would you mind if I read your poem? I want to see how it will sound if I play with it a little bit." Then I read the poem aloud, carefully, giving weight to each thought, pausing where a pause lends emphasis. Then I ask the poet and the class if they believe it helped to read the poem that way. When they agree, I hand the poem back to the poet. I might ask him to try it that way or just suggest that he practice later reading it like that.

8 A Spatial Way to Learn: Interpreting a Poem

from Kathy

Divide the class into small groups. Pass out one or more poetry selections. Invite students to take the poem or poems and decide how they should be shared with the class. Give them 10 to 15 minutes to prepare and then have each group present their interpretation to the whole class. You might suggest that they use props to enhance their presentations.

from David

I was listening to a fifth-grade student read her poem to the class and noted her clever use of sound effects. A snake hissed, a dog barked, and a girl yelled for help. I suggested that the poem might be fun if it were read by two voices. The next day I was delighted when the girl teamed up with a friend. Together they had great fun, with one reading the poem as the other chimed in with the sound effects.

In another school, each student chose a favorite poem and read it to the class in the fashion of a mini play. They had a wonderful time, moving about, gesturing, wearing a hat, or shaking a stick . . . whatever they decided was appropriate for the enactment of the poem. Even boys who normally were a bit shy in front of a group seemed to lose some inhibitions when they could clutch the book in one hand and gesture with the other.

TOCK TALK (For Two Voices)

by David L. Harrison

(Second Voice)	(First Voice)	
	TICK	TOCK
	TICK	TOCK
	TICK	TOCK
	TICK	TOCK
Clocks don't care	TICK	TOCK
	TICK	TOCK
Clocks don't care	TICK	TOCK
If you toss all night!	TICK	TOCK
Clocks don't care!	TICK	TOCK
	TICK	TOCK
Clocks don't care	TICK	TOCK
If you don't sleep tight!	TICK	TOCK
All they ever do is	TICK	TOCK
	TICK	TOCK
All night through they	TICK	TOCK
	TICK	TOCK
Cover up your head they	TICK	TOCK
	TICK	TOCK
Roll around your bed they	TICK	TOCK
	TICK	TOCK
All night long they	TICK	TOCK
	TICK	TOCK
Same old song they	TICK	TOCK
	TICK	TOCK
Same old verse they	TICK	TOCK
	TICK	TOCK
What could be worse than	TICK	TOCK
	TICK	TOCK?
	BRRRRINGGG!	

from *The Alligator in the Closet*. Copyright (c) 2003 by David L. Harrison.
Reprinted by permission of Boyds Mills Press.

⑨ Two-Voice Poetry: Adding Fun to Reading Aloud

from Kathy

Divide your class into pairs. Choose a "two-voice" poetry selection. Be sure to model this strategy first, with you taking one part and a student volunteer reading the other. Next, pass out one or more selections. Have the partners practice their poems. Later, have them take turns presenting their two-voice poetry selections in front of the class.

from David

Georgia Heard has written a number of poems for two voices. Here's one of mine that features a sleepless victim of a ticking clock. Someone who can't sleep frets all night about the unfeeling clock. For its part, the clock ticks away with the relentless regularity of a metronome.

⑩ Poetry, Art, and Writing Portfolios: Getting Acquainted

from Kathy

At the beginning of the year, my partner, Ann Connell-Allen, and I send a letter home asking students to bring in photos of their family, their home, vacations they have taken, or pets they own. We also invite them to bring in ribbons they've won, a favorite poem, or any other small item that would help us get to know them. We make certain to say that these personal artifacts will be glued and laminated onto two pieces of construction paper, creating a portfolio, and the items on the outside of the portfolio will remain there permanently. The portfolios are placed in a large plastic tub and students add their work to the folders throughout the year. At the end of the year, students take their portfolios home.

11 Prose-to-Poetry Life History: Writing What We Know

from Kathy

Invite students to think about some events in their lives that have a great deal of meaning to them. You might ask them to make a web to help them capture their thoughts. I thought about riding my bike to the small library in my hometown as a young child, on my weekly quest to find new books; living on Maui during the summer of 1966 and working as a trimmer in a pineapple cannery; and working as a ride operator at Disneyland while in college. I would select one of those ideas, write a prose piece, and then use the prose piece for inspiration for a poem.

David once wrote a story about his family returning home to Missouri at the end of World War II. He then developed a poem that was inspired by living through a frigid winter with only a coal-burning stove for heating.

12 Hook Them With Humor: Everybody Likes to Laugh

from Kathy

At the beginning of every year, I try to incorporate humorous poetry into the day. I put the poems on large pieces of colored tagboard and invite the children to either "echo read" or to read the poems with me. At this time, I also introduce humorous anthologies written by a variety of poets, and I share some of the poems from the books. It never fails. Several members of the class will ask if they can read one of the poetry books during SQUIRT (silent quiet uninterrupted independent reading time). I even find the humorous poetry books hidden in their desks and have to rescue them. They want to read these poems over and over again!

NIGHT THOUGHTS
by David L. Harrison

It's late.
Too cold to sleep.

The hot water bottle
turns my feet clammy
with its rubbery weight
like congealed gravy.

Cold surrounds my lone warm spot.
I think of snow angels.
I think of chalk outlines.
"This is where we found the frozen body."

I stare through the dark
at the coal stove,
a slumbering gnome,
potbelly full of last night's ashes.

Dad says soon we'll find something better.
Imprisoned inside my own outline,
I think my night thoughts
and wait for morning.

from Kathy

Choose a particular type of weather and invite the class to brainstorm about what makes this type of weather unique. You might want to have students use their five senses or come up with similes while brainstorming. Set the tone for a certain type of weather by playing music. CDs or cassettes with the sound of rain falling in the background could be used for rainstorms, for example, or cheerful music might depict a day filled with sunshine. You can take your class outside and savor the sunlight or the snowstorm and invite students to jot down what they notice. Another idea is to discuss onomatopoeia, using words whose sound suggests the sense (e.g., buzz, hiss). This technique is especially effective if students choose to write about the wind blowing or being in a violent thunderstorm. Mount the completed poems on construction paper and invite students to illustrate them. The poems can be hung from the ceiling or a bulletin board in the classroom, or hung on a wall to decorate the hall!

NIGHT STORM
by David L. Harrison

(First Voice)
Growling cloudy beasts go prowling
Stalking through the night,
With fiery eyes they roam the skies
Spoiling for a fight.

(Second Voice)

Thunderous roars
And lightning breath
Scare the timid
Half to death!

With tooth and claw they gnash and gnaw
And clash with roars of pain
Till fangs and scales and tips of tails
Rattle down like rain.

Lightning breath
And thunderous roars
Keep the timid
Scared indoors!

With flashing scowls they shriek and howl
Till every beast lies dead,
Their roisterous fight all through the night
Paints the morning red.

No one's frightened
Anymore
Of lightning breath
Or thunderous roar.

14 "Question" Poetry: Harnessing Natural Curiosity

from Kathy

Many times children and adults have unanswered questions about life. Poetry is the perfect vehicle to explore these questions. I introduce this lesson by putting a "question" poem on the overhead.

Georgia Heard's poem "Will We Ever See?" (at right) is a good example.

I have the whole class read the poem aloud and then ask if they notice anything that is special about this poem.

I then ask them to get out their journal or "writer's notebook," and we brainstorm other possibilities for question poems. They might start by using the words *who, what when, where,* or *why.*

Next, on the overhead, I model things I've wondered about. What will traffic be like in ten years? What type of music will be popular in the future? Will there be a cure for a certain disease?

Then I say, "In your notebooks, jot down some questions that you have pondered. They might be questions about the environment, your family, or the future."

After ten minutes or so, I ask the class to share their ideas in small groups or with the entire class. I also say, "Tonight you might want to take your notebooks home and add some ideas to your list."

I let these ideas percolate for a day or two before asking students to incorporate them into question poems.

> **WILL WE EVER SEE?**
> *by Georgia Heard*
>
> Will we ever see a tiger again,
> stalking its prey with shining eyes?
>
> Will we see the giant orangutan
> inspecting its mate for fleas?
>
> Or a California condor
> feeding on the side of a hill?
>
> Or a whooping crane
> walking softly through a salty marsh?
>
> Or hear the last of the blue whales
> singing its sad song under the deep water?

from *Creatures of the Earth, Sea, and Sky.* Copyright © 1992 by Georgia Heard. Published by Boyds Mills Press.

15 Matching Poems With Personalities: Matching What We Know With What We Think We Know

from David

Here's another fun activity involving your students in scavenger hunts through anthologies of poetry. Start a list on the board of animals to which we humans tend to assign human characteristics.

Begin with something easy, such as a turtle. Now ask your class to give you a word that describes the turtle. Some students will say "slow." Others might think of "shy," "quiet," or "patient."

That's a good start. Try another. Maybe the fox. Students may say "sly" or "smart" or "quick." More than one personality or physical trait is fine as long as each fits the general characteristics that we associate with that animal. Your list might look something like this:

Turtle	slow, shy, quiet, patient	**Bull**	angry, strong, impatient
Fox	sly, smart, quick, clever	**Dog**	faithful, playful, loud, friendly

When the list is long enough to demonstrate the idea, give your students time to copy it into their writers' notebooks and encourage them to add other animals and traits on their own.

Now comes the fun. Allow a week for every student to find at least one poem to match each animal on the list. Provide as many poetry anthologies and collections in the room as you can, but encourage your students to find poems on their own to copy into their notebooks.

Hint: The poems should stress at least one of the traits we associate with that animal.

To help maintain momentum, choose a different student each day to read a poem aloud that matches one of the animals on the list.

At the end of the week, hold a poetry jam. You name an animal and then go around the room, asking students to read poems about that animal. (Skip duplications to save time.)

This is a good way to involve students in thinking about animals and the way we give them human traits that they may or may not deserve.

An extension of this idea is to then let students write poems about an animal of their choice.

16 Visiting Poet: Creating Excitement Through Personal Visits

from Kathy

Our school invited David Harrison to visit us for an entire day. Before his arrival, I made certain that each grade level had poetry books written by David to share with their students. Our library media specialist also read David's poems to classes when they came to the library.

When David finally arrived, the students were thrilled! With his midwestern humor and his genuine love of children, he captivated his audience. He was able to relate to all children in our school from kindergarten through fifth grade because of his wide range of experiences and expertise. A good time was had by all.

17 Writing Letters to a Poet: Lessons in Correspondence

from Kathy

Last fall, my class studied poetry written by David Harrison. I made a conscious effort to include his serious poems as well as his signature humorous poems.

The culminating activity was to have each child write a letter to David. In the letter, each child was asked to make specific comments about his poems and to ask him questions.

David painstakingly responded to each child in a letter that he sent back to my class. Below is an excerpt from his letter:

October 21, 2001

Dear Mrs. Holderith's Kids,

What wonderful letters! I have read them all and feel honored to receive so many good comments and questions. Thank you!

Greg, I have never been asked how I put the groove into my poems. That's an original. I've been thinking about that one and will probably use your question when I talk to other groups because it's the sort of thing that makes a person think.

Part of the answer, I think has to do with how much of our heart goes into a poem. Read "Leaving Corky" in *The Purchase of Small Secrets* as an example of a poem that means a lot to me on a personal basis. Another one, in the same book, is "Beginner's Luck," about the time I killed a cardinal. I still remember with shame the moment when I carelessly took that bird's life for no reason, how miserable I felt.

Genna, I've written hundreds of poems and dozens of books. I'm glad that you like "Monday" and "Cow Pie Jewels." I wrote about the cow pies because the incident really happened to me. I decided to leave those little blue butterflies where they were and look for some somewhere else in a safer place.

18 Animal Poetry: Writing Descriptive Poems

from Paula Shannon, Director of Curriculum and Instruction for Littleton Public Schools, Littleton, CO

Some children benefit from having a frame to help them develop a poem. I begin this lesson on animal poetry by having the students get out a piece of paper. I ask them to divide the paper into fourths and label each section (see right).

Here is an example that Kathy wrote while she attended an in-service that I gave in the Littleton Public Schools.

Name of the animal	Describe your animal (adjectives)
Describe how it moves	Tell what it is doing

PIKA

Delicate furry mountain mouse
Scrampers over craggy rocks
Stops, listens
Chomps a few kernels of grain
Suns itself on a
chestnut rock
Pika

19 Name Know-It-All: Writing Acrostic Poems

from Kelly Huber, second-grade teacher, Littleton Public Schools, Littleton, Colorado

As a culminating activity for our "Getting to Know You" unit, we play this game. We start the game by calling out a student's name, such as Melissa. Melissa spells her name, one letter at a time. As she does this, any student may call out an attribute that describes Melissa, using words that begin with the particular letter that she is calling out at the time. For example: *M* is for *magnificent*, *E* is for *elephant* (which is her favorite animal), *L* is for *listens* carefully, *I* is for *ice cream*, and so on. It is an intriguing activity because it uses acrostics poetry in a verbal, rather than a written, form.

20 Friday Fishbowl: Memorizing Poetry!

from Ruth Nathan, third-grade teacher, Rancho Romero, Alamo, California

"Friday Fishbowl" is a time period each Friday when my class celebrates poets by reciting poems that they've memorized during the week. When a student learns a poem by heart, he or she writes the title on a paper fish and puts it into our "fishbowl."

Each Friday, we visit the library, sit in a circle, and pull a fish out of the bowl. The child selected stands and shares the memorized poem. In appreciation, students quietly snap their fingers when the child finishes the recitation. My students love this ceremony.

My class gets many ideas for poems during our daily meetings, where the leader for the day ends opening announcements with a poem of his or her choice. We often talk briefly about the poem, many times emphasizing the meaning and the word choice. My third graders enjoy all sorts of poems, from Shakespeare to Silverstein.

They've memorized so many poems that they gave the entire school a "Poetry Break." During this time, the students made a "Poetry Break" sign and visited various rooms, interrupting classes to share a few poems with them. (I had gotten permission from the teachers, of course.)

21 A Practical Poetry Idea: Creating a Sense of Teamwork

from Susan Dalton, language arts teacher on special assignment,
Littleton Public Schools, Littleton, Colorado

When discussing poetry, bring the class close together so everyone can see the piece. Put the poem on an overhead transparency. (It can be a student-written poem or a published poem.) Have the class read the poem aloud. Ask the children to point out features that are found in the poem, such as word choice, strong verbs, and descriptive language. As they give suggestions, write their responses on the overhead. After the discussion, students can begin to write poems of their own, possibly incorporating some of the features found in the model poems.

Always close your sessions with a sharing and celebration time. Above all, have fun with poetry!

22 Selecting a Topic: A Great Way to Get Started

from Merrillyn Brooks Kloefkorn, educational consultant, Lakewood, Colorado

Children often have trouble writing poetry because they think it must rhyme.

Like	Dislike	Fear	Want

Added to this, they have trouble selecting a topic. Once the rhyming myth has been dispelled, the following activity will allow young writers to zero in on a topic about which they have strong feelings and knowledge.

Give each student the above graphic organizer. Ask them to list everything they can think of that they really like. When they have finished the first list, have them proceed to each of the other three categories. Be sure to give the students adequate time for each list. When all four lists have been completed, ask the students to review their lists of "likes" and circle the one choice they like the most. Repeat this procedure with each category. When all of them have finished making their choices, go through the four categories, giving students an opportunity to discuss the reasons for their choices. Students now have four topics about which they have strong feelings and knowledge. It is time for them to write their poems.

23 "I Hope You Dance" Activity: Learning Through Modeling

—Song by Mark D. Saunders and Tia Sillers —Sung by LeeAnn Womack
from Valerie McCarthy-Smith, fourth-fifth grade teacher,
Aurora Quest School, Aurora, Colorado

Begin by sharing "I Hope You Dance" on CD or tape. You might want to copy the lyrics on chart paper or an overhead so students can read along.

After sharing this beautiful poem with the students, have them respond to the following questions in writing:

1. In one sentence, what do you think this poem is about? What message is the writer trying to give the reader?

2. Tell about one part of the poem in which you made a personal connection.

3. What is your favorite part of this piece? Tell me why you like it.

4. Write another line for this poem. Begin it like one of the lines in the poem. (For example: I hope . . ., May you . . ., When you . . ., Promise . . ., Never . . ., Whenever . . .)

24 Poetry Time: Creating A Classroom of Poetry Lovers

from Vicki Ogden, assistant principal, Ridgeview Elementary, Liberty, Missouri

During the seven years that I taught fifth grade, I established an end-of-the-day "Poetry Time." I'd been looking for a way to expose my students to poetry and help them learn to love this genre of writing.

To initiate this program, I explained that the end of each day would be

Poetry Time; students could sign up to read a poem to the class by writing their names in the corner of the chalkboard where I had created a daily sign-up chart.

I put up three days at a time and made three slots for each day. I reminded students that before they read their poems to the class, they would need to practice reading them aloud.

For the first couple of days, I modeled Poetry Time by sharing some of my own favorites. We talked about using expression in our voices and making sure we knew all the words. I encouraged searching for poetry in our classroom collection of poetry books or in others found in the library or at home.

I was amazed at the popularity of Poetry Time. Students couldn't wait to sign up to read! So many wanted to participate that I had to set a limit. No one could read more than twice a week. This became a coveted time of the day that everyone eagerly anticipated.

Visits to the library often included searches for new poems to share. Many poems were read to the class repeatedly, but students never got tired of hearing them again and again.

Aside from the appreciation for poetry, my fifth graders became better readers and writers. During our writers' workshop, they wanted to write poems, and they experimented with different forms.

Throughout the years I taught, Poetry Time was a hit. It became a daily ritual, one that my students wouldn't let me miss.

Poetry Focus Lessons: Learning the Basics of Poetry

from Kathy

I incorporate poetry into my curriculum throughout the year, but you can emphasize poetry in a special poetry unit. During the unit, you can focus on different types of poems and the powerful lessons poetry can teach.

I begin the unit by giving each child a three-prong folder, which they decorate, and a "Poetry Log" sheet. I tell them, "Please keep the Poetry Log in your poetry folder and use it to record the poems and/or poetry books that you read. After you record the poem, you might want to make a brief comment about how you felt about the poem."

Each day during the unit, I use focus lessons to teach some aspect of poetry. On the next page is a list of possible focus lessons that you might find useful.

Possible Focus Lessons:

This is a list of focus lessons I gleaned from Georgia Heard after attending a workshop she gave and reading her book *For the Good of the Earth and Sun*.

1. Lines in poetry may be long and thin or fat and wide.

2. Line breaks serve a purpose.

3. Reread your poems to decide where line breaks should occur.

4. Verbs are the engines that keep your poem moving. (Have a "verb search." Work in small groups or individually to find poems that incorporate strong verbs in them.)

5. Poetry usually has rhythm to it.

6. Repeat a line in a poem in order to emphasize it.

7. A poem sometimes concludes with a "surprise" ending.

8. Good poets sometimes repeat a word or phrase two or three times to emphasize something.

9. Some poems contain alliteration.

10. Poems sometimes ask questions.

11. Some poems are "list" poems.

This is just a beginning. Many of the poetry focus lessons that I've developed have come from observation, innovation, and listening to my students. As Georgia Heards says, "The listening is everything." I concur.

CHAPTER 2

The World in a Grain of Sand:

Exploring Ourselves And Our World

The right words and the right number of words are not easily achieved.
—Jean Karl

Being creative takes time.
—Kathy Holderith

Part of growing up involves learning who we are, where we fit in, and how we relate to others. Understanding our thoughts and feelings about those issues is a complicated process. Poetry, the most personal form of writing, provides many opportunities for young people to explore the world and their place in it.

This chapter relates to the need for self-expression by encouraging curiosity, introducing journal-keeping, offering ways to find ideas, and demonstrating that writing isn't so mysterious after all.

FROM KATHY'S CLASSROOM

What Is a Citrullus Vulgaris?

Using Our Senses

Poet's Note

I love the sounds that long words make. Coleoptera *is a fine example. It rolls around on the tongue with an impressive recipe of vowels you can nearly taste. It makes the common beetle sound fancy enough to take dancing. Butterflies don't need much help but* lepidoptera *lends them a royal air. So does* Papilionidae, *the family name for swallowtail butterflies. Writers in general and poets in particular fall in love with language. We savor words like chocolate lovers and should be grateful that our figures don't suffer from our binges.*

So naturally I would love Kathy's segment on Citrullus vulgaris *even if all she had her kids do was learn how to pronounce the words and set off like butterfly collectors in search of others worth keeping. Trading nets and pins for journals and pens, her students would soon discover that words are more diverse than all the butterflies and beetles they'll ever see.*

I'm for anything that stimulates observation and awakening the senses, which this exercise does very well. But it goes beyond the search to identify new words. It encourages students to carefully observe their subject and seek strong verbs that match what they see. Whether your area is blessed with Citrullus vulgaris, Danaus plexippus, *or* Tribolium confusum, *I think what's going on here is more than just a lot of fun. It's an important step for developing young scientists and writers.*

Focus Lesson:

Good writers use sensory details and active verbs.

■ ■ ■ ■ ■ ■ ■

A cinquain poem is basically a five-line stanza form of poetry. I have found that at the beginning of the year, young poets benefit greatly from using the special structure of a particular form of cinquain poem with rules about what each line

Materials Suggested

- Sign entitled "What Is a *Citrullus Vulgaris?*"

- Sign entitled "This Is a *Citrullus Vulgaris.*"

- "Observing the Watermelon" reproducible (pg 33)

- Cinquain Graphic Organizer reproducible with instructions on how to write a selected form of cinquain poem, a model poem, and a cinquain poetry frame (pg 34)

- One large watermelon

- One paper plate per student for holding a slice of watermelon

of their poem should contain. This sets a positive tone; children feel successful and are inspired to write poetry for the rest of the year.

This unit also includes several extension activities that can be easily implemented.

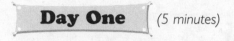 (5 minutes)

Setting the Stage

As my students walk into class, I ask them if they notice anything new. One says, "Yes, I notice that there's a sign." I ask the class what the sign says. No one can pronounce the last two words on the sign, so I say aloud, "What is a *Citrullus vulgaris?*" One boy, Ben, says that it sounds like something Latin.

I say, "Yes, Ben, you're on the right track."

I add, "Your homework for tonight is to try to find out the meaning of those two words. You might want to use a dictionary, your computer, or any other source that you can think of." This quick introduction intrigues students and builds motivation for the lesson that follows.

Day Two (60 minutes)

Generating Sensory Details

The next day, several of my students run up to me. "I know what it means!" they yell. I ask them not to divulge their answer to anyone, except me. I call them up to my desk one by one and ask them to whisper it into my ear. (Yes, they do have the correct answer!)

I ask students to close their eyes. I set the watermelon on a round table with a sign that says, "I am a *Citrullus vulgaris.*" Then I ask them to open their eyes. Boy, is the class excited now!

I pass out the Observing the Watermelon reproducible (page 33). I say, "Today you are going to use your senses to carefully describe the *Citrullus vulgaris.*"

Next, I cut up the watermelon into pieces, place them on paper plates and pass them out to the class. I tell the class to use only their senses of *seeing* and *smelling* first and quickly jot down all the words that they can think of on their reproducible. I have an overhead of the reproducible, and I jot down some of their ideas as they share them. Then they proceed to *feeling* the watermelon, and they are allowed to *taste* it. As they taste it, I ask them to think of all the action verbs that they can and list them on their sheet. (*Hint: Your action words should end with *-ing.)

Name *Elizabeth Zasowski*   Date *Sept. 15, 2002*

Observing the Watermelon

Use this sheet to record your observations of the watermelon.

Watermelons are (what does it look like?) *Ruby Red triangle*

Watermelons smell *Garden of fruit*

Watermelons taste *squishy, watery*

Action words (verbs) used to describe you eating your watermelon: *Chewing, smushing, swallowing*

How do you feel as you are eating your watermelon? *I feel fantastic when I eat my watermelon.*

I end this portion of the lesson by saying, "Please keep your Observing the Watermelon sheet in your desk. You will use it again soon."

Day Three *(45–60 minutes)*

Teaching the Focus Lesson and Drafting the Poems

The next day, I begin class by asking, "What is a cinquain poem?" Usually, no one knows. I pass out copies of our Cinquain Graphic Organizer, which includes a model poem and a cinquain *Citrullus vulgaris* "poetry frame" (see page 34). I place the reproducible on the overhead and begin the lesson by saying, "Our cinquain poem has a special form. Each line has specific types of words. Skim and scan the sheet. Who can tell me what goes on the first line?"

Emily excitedly raises her hand and says, "It is the subject. It tells the reader what the poem is about."

"Excellent answer, Emily. This first line is also the title of your poem. Who can tell me what the subject of our poem will be?"

Matt answers, "I think it is going to be a watermelon or a *Citrullus vulgaris*."

"Yes, I can tell that you've been listening, Matt. Thank you for your input."

The lesson continues. "Now I would like everyone to look at the model poem. It was written by Hayden Brink, one of my former students. Let's read it together."

After we finish reading the poem, we continue to go over what each line in our special form of a cinquain contains.

I say, "Using our model poem, who can tell me the two words that the poet used to describe his slice of watermelon?"

"Hayden used *green* and *sweet*," mentions Melissa.

"Fantastic, Melissa!"

Using Hayden's poem, we continue to discuss what each line contains. After that, I pass out two more models of watermelon poems and say, "Right now, I'd like us to read these poems aloud. The first one we're going to recite together, and for the second one I will say a line and then you will echo-read." I try to have more than one model so my class can see that the poetry possibilities are endless.

I announce, "Now comes the fun and creative part of the lesson. Look carefully at your Cinquain Graphic Organizer. At the bottom of the sheet is a special poetry frame. Please get out your Observing the Watermelon sheet. You are ready to write about your watermelon." On their observation sheet, I ask them to write:

> Watermelon
>
> Green, sweet
>
> Tasting, savoring, dissolving
>
> It makes me feel like I'm eating a one-of-a-kind meal
>
> *Citrullus vulgaris*
>
> by Hayden Brink

first line: a title

second line: two adjectives describing their watermelon

third line: three action verbs describing them eating their *Citrullus vulgaris*

fourth line: how it makes them feel, and

fifth line: the title again or a synonym (or synonyms) for their title.

I give them poetic license on the last line. They can write a two-word synonym, if they wish.

I say, "This is your rough draft, so just get your thoughts down on paper."

At this time I circulate and make sure they understand how to write their poems.

Day Four (*20–30 minutes during the next day or two*)

Revising

Early the next day, I ask my class to get out their Cinquain Graphic Organizer sheets and join me at the easel. I say, "This morning I'm going to write a watermelon poem and you're going to help me revise it. Look over your sheet. Who can tell me what goes on the first line?"

Natalie says, "You have to write the title." So I write *Watermelon* and underline it.

Invite students to mount their final copy on paper watermelons made from green and red construction paper, as shown on the bulletin board above. Vines made out of paper and twisted with a pencil complete the scene. Or you can assemble the mounted poems into a shape book for the whole class to enjoy.

"What comes next?" I ask.

"Two words that describe the watermelon," Rachel responds.

I add *green, juicy* to the next line and say, "When we revise, we sometimes add words, change their order, or take them out. Is there another way that I could describe my watermelon?"

"Yes," says Ben, who possesses an amazing vocabulary. "You could say, *succulent, emerald.*"

I write *succulent, emerald* under *green, juicy.* Now I say, "You might want me to change the order of the words." I place *emerald, succulent* and *juicy, green* on the list, too.

"Now class, we're going to share each of the possibilities for the first two lines of my poem aloud and you're going to vote on which choice sounds the best." The class decides on *emerald, succulent* and that's what I write.

I continue the process of having the class help me with each line, and they do an outstanding job.

Next, I ask everyone to go to their seats, get out the rough drafts of their poems, and select a partner to read with them. I say that it's important to share the drafts out loud so that the partner can give suggestions. If necessary, the child then makes revisions. After that, I ask the students to circle words that might be misspelled. At this time, I have the class sign up for a final editing with me.

The final results are as refreshing as . . . well . . . watermelons!

Math Connections

(*The two math activities should be done *before* the watermelon is cut up.)

Estimation: Weight Before I cut the watermelon up, I have my students estimate how much they think the watermelon weighs. I usually let each child hold the watermelon before estimating; I ask students to record their estimates on a sticky note. I make a graph showing the range of the estimates and invite each student to place his or her sticky note on the graph in the appropriate place. Then I have one student stand on the scale. I record his or her weight without the watermelon and once again holding the watermelon. I have my students subtract the difference in order to find out how much the watermelon really weighs.

Estimation: Circumference I have students estimate the circumference of the watermelon using a piece of string. After each child has cut a piece of string showing his or her estimate, I place a piece of string around the watermelon and cut it. Next, I make a string graph using butcher paper and double-sided masking tape. The students place their piece of string in the proper place for overestimating, underestimating, or estimating correctly. I then discuss the results and have them write about the activity in their math logs.

Extend the Learning: Leaf Cinquain Poems

Many times when a poetic form or a new concept is taught, the students complete one assignment and the form is never revisited. This year after my students had written their *Citrullus vulgaris* poems, I asked them to bring in leaves. After examining their leaves carefully, I asked them to use their senses to compose cinquain "Leaves" poems. With this topic, I had them watch me drop leaves as I was standing on a chair. We brainstormed verbs

Materials Suggested

Weighing the Watermelon:

- One scale
- One piece of butcher paper for graphing the weights
- One sticky note per child, used to estimate the weight

Graphing the Circumference of the Watermelon

- One large ball of string
- One large piece of red or green butcher paper for graphing the circumference of the watermelon

Leaf Poems

Leaves
Sleek, sunset orange
Twisting, spinning, zooming
Makes me feel like dancing
Lovely spinners
                    by McKenna Brink

Leaves
Smooth, mahogany
Flipping, zooming, flying
Makes me feel warm
Little parachutes
                    by Khalil Arcady

Leaves
Jagged, pale peach
Swooping, zooming, diving
Makes me feel wonderful
Beautiful drifters
                    by Matt Sabey

as I continued to let go of the leaves. (You should have heard the strong verbs that they came up with!)

Then I asked them to stand up and drop a few of their own leaves (without standing on their chairs). The students realized that they had to be very selective in their choice of verbs. The verbs that worked in the watermelon poems were not appropriate for their leaves poems. The poems were highly successful because the children already had a comfort level and a background knowledge base. The completed poems were mounted on fall-colored construction paper and the children decorated their finished products with leaf borders.

The Poet's Approach

As a visiting author, I've abbreviated Kathy's *Citrullus vulgaris* idea with fun results. My schedule goes like this:

 **Day One** *(5 minutes)*

Setting the Stage

After a brief discussion about the importance of being a good observer, I write on the board, *Citrullus vulgaris.* I announce, in a conspiratorial voice, "By tomorrow your job is to find out what a *Citrullus vulgaris* is." Fingers to my lips, I say, "You must not tell another soul what you learn, except me."

All eyes are on me. "And this is what *I'm* going to do: If I possibly can, I will track down and trap a wild *Citrullus vulgaris*! Yes! I will capture one, and I will bring it here to this very room!"

"And do you know what we are going to do then? We are going to measure it. We are going to weigh it. Then we are going to cut it up and eat it! And after that, we are going to write poems about what we have observed!"

Appropriate responses (greatly encouraged):

"Oooo!"

"Oh no!"

"Do we have to?"

"Yuck!"

"Are you serious?"

I continue, "I have never been more serious in my entire life. Now remember your job! By tomorrow, seek out the true identity of the wily *Citrullus vulgaris.*"

Day Two (30 minutes)

Generating Sensory Details

Before the students come in, I set the watermelon on the floor in a corner and hide it beneath a large cardboard carton that is clearly labeled STAY AWAY FROM THIS BOX and THIS BOX EATS CHILDREN!

One brow arched, I stand before the group and wait. Most faces look smugly in-the-know; a few are blank. One by one, students notice the box. It becomes a strong magnet that tugs at their attention.

"What's that?" they giggle.

"That," I inform them, not bothering to hide my pride, "is exactly what I promised you."

"You mean the . . . "

"Shh! You'll wake it up!"

I approach the box with enormous caution. Signaling for absolute silence (which is definitely not hard to obtain), I advance the last few feet on tiptoe. The room is still. I reach out. My hands rest on the box. I take a deep breath and hold it.

I jerk the box off the floor and leap backward!

Everyone flinches even as they laugh at the watermelon resting peacefully on the floor.

After a bit more fun, we get down to business. We guess at the distance around the melon. If there is time, we use Kathy's string method. The students take turns lifting the melon and guessing at its weight. If a scale is available, we weigh it. Enthusiasm runs high.

A teacher or librarian volunteers to be our recorder, and we get busy observing our *Citrullus vulgaris* and describing what we see. I only let them describe the outside. The inside comes later.

Round (nearly/almost)
Heavy
Light green at the bottom
Green stripes running up and down
Stem on top
Smooth
Shiny
Scars and blemishes
Scratches
Not perfect

I tell them, "By the next time we meet, I expect you to bring poems you've written about food. You can write about the watermelon or about anything else you like to eat or don't like to eat. I don't care what you choose as long as you observe it carefully and use what you have learned in your poem."

Because my time with the students will be too brief to get into particular poetic forms, I tell them that I don't care if their poems rhyme or not, or how long or short they are. I say that they may write as a class or individually. I set no rules. I tell them, "Just write!"

I dismiss the group to take the watermelon back to their class where they will have a chance to observe how their captive tastes.

Day Three *(30–45 minutes)*

Sharing the Poems

We meet and set right to work reading poems. There are many who want to share. Most have written about the watermelon, but others have decided to write about other sorts of food. Here are samples from one group:

Student Poems

Poems written as a class by Mrs. Moran's third-graders in Malaysia:

WATERMELON

In the farmer's field
Citrullus vulgaris grows
in the summertime.

Watermelon
Citrullus vulgaris
Eat it up!
Heavy, smooth, juicy, striped
Delicious

I HATE CHILI
by Taylor Jane Fifield, Australia

I hate chili.
It is hot and spicy.
It hides in my food.
Red, green, yellow, and brown.
I hate chili.
Yuck, yuck, yuck.

THE STINKY WINKY WATERMELON
by Theresa Ahrens, Germany

I hate stinky winky watermelon.
I hate stinky winky watermelon.
It has a stinky winky taste.
It even has a stinky winky smell.
It's red inside.
Yuck, Yuck, Yuck!
I hate stinky winky watermelon.
I hate stinky winky watermelon

Observing the Watermelon

Use this sheet to record your observations of the watermelon.

Watermelons are (what does it look like?) _____

_____

_____

_____

Watermelons smell _____

_____

_____

_____

Watermelons taste _____

_____

_____

_____

Action words (verbs) used to describe you eating your watermelon:

_____

_____

_____

_____

How do you feel as you are eating your watermelon?

_____

_____

_____

_____

_____

Cinquain Graphic Organizer

A cinquain poem has five lines. This cinquain has a special form:

Line 1:   One or two words that name the subject (this is the title of the poem)
Line 2:   Two adjectives that describe the subject
Line 3:   Three verbs showing action that pertains to the subject
Line 4:   Several words giving your reaction to the subject
Line 5:   Repeat of the title or a synonym that pertains to the subject

Example

Watermelon

Green, sweet

Tasting, savoring, dissolving

It makes me feel like I'm eating a one-of-a-kind meal

Citrullus vulgaris

By Hayden Brink

Using the poetry frame below, refer to your Observing the Watermelon sheet, and write a cinquain about your *Citrullus vulgaris*.

Line 1: _____

Line 2: _____

Line 3: _____

Line 4: _____

Line 5: _____

FROM KATHY'S CLASSROOM

Writers' Notebooks, Journals, Folders

Collecting Our Thoughts

Throughout our book we refer to writers' notebooks, folders, forms, journals, and other methods of keeping track of ideas. We frequently encourage their use when students are gathering information that will help them write poems. The ideas in this mini unit will help students see the value of keeping a writer's notebook and give them ideas for getting started.

Finding the Right Format

At the beginning of the year, I send a letter home inviting children to talk with their parents about what type of writer's notebook they would like to use during the year. In the letter I say that selecting a special notebook is a very personal decision. Some people enjoy writing in a spiral notebook, while others prefer writing in a more formal journal. I tell them that the most important thing is that they feel comfortable with their choice. The children have at least a week to bring their writer's notebooks in. I also share my journal with them and tell them that I prefer writing in a journal that doesn't have lines. I feel strongly that it is important that they know that I am a writer and that my notebook is precious to me.

> Writing . . . is an extension of an author's own real life; and in some cases it is more than that, it is the place where he most truly lives.
>
> –Jean Karl

Poet's Note

A journal is anything you can write in. No need to be fancy. Messy is fine. Some writers draw sketches and tape articles and leaves and ticket stubs among the pages. I've seen journals bulging like over-stuffed suitcases with bits of this and that barely managing to hang on, or in. Adults usually work out their own methods. Kids will, too, given enough time and encouragement.

Dividing the Notebook With Tabs

Some teachers have focus lessons at the beginning of the year on how students might want to divide their notebook into categories using tabs. You can assign the categories or students can develop their own. Possible categories include short stories, poetry, brainstorming on writing topics, and vocabulary words. If students want to use tabs, the important thing to teach them is to leave an adequate number of pages between each category.

Using the Notebook to Collect Ideas and Inspire Writing

Journals or writers' notebooks give children a place to brainstorm, a place to record keen observations using their senses during a science lesson in the classroom or while they are on a nature walk. In our busy world, it acts as a vehicle for slowing us down and letting us reflect. Journals may be used for vocabulary development, for making webs, for categorizing things, to play with language, and to record focus lessons. They are a place to write hopes, dreams, and thoughts. Writers' notebooks can be incorporated into every curricular area.

Once students develop the journal habit, the act of keeping track of ideas that interest them becomes a pleasant activity. At first, students may need us to model for them what we mean by keeping a journal (or file or sack or box or drawer!) to preserve interesting thoughts and ideas. If teachers and parents lead the way, students won't take long to get the idea.

A notebook is private property. How the proprietor manages the property is his or her own business. That delicious sense of absolute freedom is one of the most important ingredients.

In the preface to her book Speaking of Journals, Paula Graham writes, "Keeping a journal is living a wide-awake life. Whatever its name— notebook, sketchbook, log, daybook, diary, or journal— the blank book we fill with bits and pieces of our lives affirms us and validates our experiences." Paula quotes from Lucy Calkins on her work with young journal keepers: "Even if youngsters are just at the stage of beginning to collect bits of their lives, it's enormously helpful for them to have a farsighted vision of the role these entries might eventually play in creating finished pieces of writing."

Poet's Note

My first efforts at journal keeping began during my butterfly collecting days. Spotting the year's first, freshly emerged butterfly was an exciting event, a sure sign that spring was on its way at last, a good omen well worth recording. Notes, observations, and ideas tucked away in folders and journals become the writer's storehouse of treasure, his gold, or, more precisely, his flux to spin into gold.

I love exploring among my journals and idea files, pulling up this article or that picture and holding it to the light of my

*imagination to see if anything wants to shine through. If nothing does,
I move on to the next item. Once I pulled out an article about a baby
pig that escaped his pen on a farm near Denver and made it into the
suburbs. He had quite a time until two police officers captured him
in the parking lot of a Shakey's Pizza Parlor. That article inspired my
picture book Piggy Wiglet and the Great Adventure.*

> *It felt so good to be a pig
> That Piggy Wiglet danced a jig!
> He kicked his heels and flipped his tail
> And squirmed beneath the bottom rail,
> Then trotted off to have some fun—
> To play all day and chase the sun.*

Selected Contents of One of David's Writing Folders

Numerous other books, articles, essays, and poems trace their origins back to my journals. Here are samples of ideas from just one of many fat folders.

1. An article about coyotes and their danger to domestic cats.

2. An article about how animals communicate with one another and with humans.

3. Figures I obtained from a phone book about how many writers are listed compared to people in other professions.

4. A dozen pages of notes from a trip to Alaska. Example: "Ground was spongy, nearly covered by lichen. Blueberries were slightly sour, but they were everywhere. Limbs of many trees were covered with moss so that they looked slipcovered in padded green sleeves. A young squirrel looked at us from eye level, unafraid, curious. No other living thing seen or heard. Reminded us of Tolkien's haunted forests."

5. A list of unusual town names: Embarrass, Minnesota; Why, Arizona; Cabbage Patch, California.

6. Notes made on a plane just after takeoff: "Looking down as low sun casts long shadows across fields. Rolls of hay, cattle, all throw long shadows."

7. Did you know there are one million worms in an acre of land? Or that they churn up twenty to forty tons of topsoil per acre per year?

Those tidbits are jotted on a scrap of paper in my files, which prompted this bit of spontaneous silliness:

> Worms eat tons of dirt a year,
> They're going to eat it all I fear!

Ten Ways to Jump-Start the Journal Habit

Here are ten ways to help students get started making records of what they think might be worth keeping. You can add plenty of your own. It might be a good idea to send the list home and encourage the whole family to add to it or to start journals of their own.

1. Take a nature walk and describe your thoughts in your journal.

2. Go through a newspaper or magazine and clip or describe articles that look interesting.

3. Describe in your journal the way a cat or dog walks, eats, sleeps, and plays.

4. Write down the most interesting thing you did today.

5. Write down the most interesting thing you saw today.

   Here's an example of a poem that grew easily from the most interesting thing I saw one rainy day. I was sitting in my house, looking out the window at the backyard, when a sparrow landed on a lawn chair. After a moment the little bird appeared to realize he was getting wet. With an impatient twitch, he flew into a nearby tree that provided some protection from the steady rain. I wrote:

   > Sparrow got his feathers wet,
   > Didn't like it not a bit,
   > Shook his head and flew away,
   > Found a tree and there he stayed.

6. Read a favorite poem and write down what you liked best.

7. Describe a poem you would like to write.

8. Pick a word and make a list of all the other words you can think of that sound the same.

9. Describe your mother/father/brother/sister/friend/teacher.

10. Make a list of your favorite things to eat.

Poet's Note

Some of the teachers I've met say that when they retire they'll write a book about their amazing experiences in the classroom. I advise them to begin tucking away those experiences as they occur and not wait 25 years and trust them to memory.

FROM DAVID'S TRAVELS

Where Do You Get Your Ideas?

"Where do you get your ideas?" Writers hear that question more than any other. Or versions of it: "How do you know what to write about?" "How do you get started?" "What made you think of that?"

The answer surprises a lot of people. I tell them that you can write about anything. Ideas are as thick as needles on a pine tree. Writing is what you do to make your subject fascinating to read about.

We need to give young writers freedom of choice as often as possible so they can write about a subject they like. And also, as often as possible, we need to give them a regular time and place to do their writing. A writer needs to feel like he's "going to work" in a familiar place and at a regular time. Ideas tend to flow better when we're wearing our writer's hat.

Here's a list of ideas from ten sources as examples of how quickly we can generate writing possibilities. Share them with your students, and let the writing begin!

> Nothing is more dangerous than an idea when it's the only one you have.
>
> –Emile Chartier
>
> The best way to get a good idea is to get a lot of ideas.
>
> –Linus Pauling

1   First Thing That Comes to Mind

Quick! Pick a word! Tile? That's as good as any. Now start listing everything you can think of that involves the floor.
How old is tile?
Who invented tile?
What is tile made of?
How do they get so many colors into each piece of tile?
Where did these tiles come from?
Who laid them on our floor?
How much training do you need to do that?
When were they laid?
How many students have sat on these tiles?
Where are those students today?

That's ten quick ideas about the classroom floor. They involve history, manufacturing, skilled labor, and even stories about other students.

2   Chain Reaction Thinking

Start with an observation, then go wherever your imagination takes you. See that sunset? It looks like a fire way out on the horizon. What sort of fire would glow like that? A forest fire! I hope the animals are okay! I can almost feel the heat and imagine the panic from here. What if a brave old buck deer with an injured leg (maybe from a hunting accident?) is out there, struggling heroically to lead his family to safety through those raging flames?

3 Take Things Literally

Look down the hall. Is it just me or do things look smaller down there? Maybe children at that end really are tiny! We must look big to them! Maybe they're afraid of us. They may have developed myths about the giants who live at our end of the hall. Should we send them a note to tell them we're actually quite friendly? Maybe we should appoint a goodwill ambassador to the Land of the Little People, and invite them to send one to us. Perhaps we'll learn more about one another's cultures. We might even have certain things in common! (Maybe we could exchange poems about each other.)

4 Make Something Bigger Than Life

Have you ever had the hiccups? There are all sorts of tricks that are supposed to cure them. Like holding your breath. Drinking water hanging upside down. Breathing into a paper bag. Having someone scare you. What if you put all that into a poem? But to make it more exciting, pretend the victim is a giant! So when he hiccups, apples fall off trees. Soup bowls bounce off tables. Babies wake up and start crying. The giant tries everything. But nothing works. Except for one thing! Now all you have to do is figure out what cures the giant's hiccups. And, oh yes, write a poem about him.

5 Find Something Really Old (No, not your teacher!)

How about imagining the oldest tree in the world? He stands there, twisted and bare, like a balding old man bent by arthritis. Lightning has split his bark during a long and sometimes dangerous life. Let's make him a bristlecone pine, the oldest living thing on our planet. When Columbus discovered his "New World," our bristlecone had been standing here for more than a thousand years!

So what does such an ancient plant have to tell us? Remember, he's old but he's never traveled. Not one inch. Maybe he's always wanted to move three feet closer to the edge of the bluff for a better view. Or back six feet so the noisy crows would stop nesting in his branches. But, of course, he can't.

Can you make up a poem about this old guy and his life?

6 Junk Mail and Catalogs

I flip through the pages of a catalog and spot an elderly woman sitting alone on the top step of her back porch. I make up a story about her. I decide she lives alone and has lost her hearing. She used to love to feed birds, but now she's too poor to buy food for them. So she sits on her porch and tries to remember the sweetness of the sound of birdsong. To the left is the sad poem I wrote about the woman in the catalog. Maybe you will write poems about her, too.

THE SOUNDS OF MEMORY

by David L. Harrison

She sits alone
listening to sounds
of memory,

Of birds eagerly
trading sweet songs
for seeds that drip
like musical notes
from slender fingers.

Gone, all gone—
the notes,
the seeds,
the songs—

She shuts her eyes
and listens to
the fading sounds
of memory.

7 Explore for Ideas

Take a walk and look for ideas to write about. What about that harmless caterpillar, all puffed up and dangerous-looking to scare off hungry birds? Or the beetle in a hurry that scurries across the path? Maybe the clouds shaped like sheep? The sweet smell of some sort of flower? The tiny hole in the ground? It's hard to write fast enough to capture all the ideas we'll find along the sidewalk or on the playground or down the hall or in the library or in the backyard or on a camping trip or on the bus. We just have to go exploring for them!

8 Talk to a Butterfly

Butterflies are amazing, gentle creatures and everyone loves to watch them. But how much do you know about them? If you were going to talk to a butterfly, what would you ask?

How many eggs do you lay?	Did other insects tease you?
Did you mind being a caterpillar?	What happened inside your chrysalis?
Do you eat anything?	Where did your wings come from?
How do you do it?	How long will you live?

Got enough answers yet to write a poem? Well, just keep talking to that butterfly until you do!

9 Favorite Subject

What do you like to think about, talk about, eat, play, or do? Well then, write about that! Write a poem about eating mashed potatoes or playing soccer or laughing with friends or playing with toy cars. Whatever you like to do makes a wonderful subject to write about.

10 Read!

The very best place to find ideas is to read what other people have written about. Get out your favorite book and make up a poem about the story. Or a character you like. It will be like writing a poem about an old friend because you already know a lot about him or her.

These ten ways to get started are just a beginning. You can add many more of your own. You can post the growing list and/or copy it to keep in your student writer's notebook.

EXTENSION IDEA . . . .

You can keep this section bookmarked and refer to it throughout the year. Depending on what you are teaching, most of these idea starters can be adapted to the subject at hand.

Mini Unit Three

FROM DAVID'S TRAVELS

Poems Around the House

Putting Observation to Work

Focus Lesson:
Good writers observe everyday objects and write about them in their own ways.

▪ ▪ ▪ ▪ ▪ ▪ ▪

Now that we've given students a little practice looking for ideas, this mini unit challenges them to put their powers of observation to work. They learn that good writing doesn't have to be about something exotic and far away. It can start much closer to home. Young writers discover the fun of turning a desk or the carpet or even the cat into a poem. And in the process, they continue to develop their skills of observation.

Readers like themes. Sometimes I choose a theme—such as school, family, or nature—and begin a book by making a list of everything I can think of about that subject. Before writing *Somebody Catch My Homework*, I listed cafeteria food, homework, the class clown, taking tests, show-and-tell, getting in trouble, oversleeping, missing the bus, and several other ideas about school. Then I chose items from the list that appealed to me the most. Some of the others were harder to relate to, and those poems did not turn out as well.

This exercise is designed to help students learn to look around them for subjects to write about. Making lists is a simple and effective way to begin.

Materials Suggested

@ Board or easel

@ Writers' notebooks

@ Poems: "Cats," by Eleanor Farjeon; "Baby Spider" and "Life's Not Fair!" by David L. Harrison (page 46)

Day One (30 minutes)

Warming Up

You might begin by saying, "Get out your writer's notebook and make a new heading called 'Things Around The Classroom.' You have five minutes to look around the room and make a list of what you see."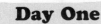

When the time is up, have your students take turns reading items from their lists. You don't need to record these on the board or easel unless you plan to ask students to write poems based on the list. This exercise is meant to be a warm-up.

Now you can have a discussion on the importance of learning to write about the everyday things in our lives, things that many professional writers use as inspiration. "A good place to start," you can tell students, "is where you spend a lot of your time. School, for example. And home."

Now read the poems provided (page 46) and hold similar, quick discussions after each. After Eleanor Farjeon's "Cats," ask how many students have dogs or cats at home. Could they write about them? "Baby Spider" reminds us that we aren't the only ones who live in our homes. We share our habitat with any number of smaller creatures. Some, like dogs or goldfish, depend on us to take care of them. Others live their lives quietly and independently from our own. "Life's Not Fair!" demonstrates that humor can be found in unexpected places.

Conclude this session by asking everyone to look around their house and bring to class a list of what they see there.

Day Two *(30 minutes or less)*

Planning the Poems

Now it's time to make a master list on the board or easel. Ask students to read from their lists while you record the items. As you go, you may try to arrange items loosely into groups such as "kitchen," "bedroom," "living room," or perhaps "food," "animals," "objects." That can also be done later if you want to have class input.

When you have completed the master list, pick out a word or phrase and ask the class to brainstorm ways to write a poem based on that subject. It helps to write the word on the board and list beneath it various suggestions from your students. Like this:

```
Kitchen Table
    Family eating together
    Doing homework
    Working puzzles
    Cat taking a nap
    Dad/Mom paying bills
```

This is a good opportunity to stress that writers take their time at this stage. They don't write about the first idea they have. Sometimes it pays to think about a subject for a while to see how many ideas turn up. Point to the kitchen table example on the board to show how many ways there can be to write about the same piece of furniture.

At the end of this session, announce that each student should choose something to write about. "But don't rush into the writing yet," you can remind them. "First, make a list of ways you might choose to handle your subject. For next time, bring the subject from the list and some ideas on how you might write about it."

Day Three (20 minutes or less)

Writing the Poems

Ask students to take turns telling the class the subject they've selected and the ways they've listed to write about it.

This is a good time to have some fun. Keep the session light to encourage even more creative thinking. Look for chances to laugh appreciatively and congratulate students for original approaches. Here are a few examples contributed during such sessions:

> Dirty dishes
> Guinea pig
> Shampoo
> Stuffed deer head in Dad's study
> Baby gecko
> Easter card from third grade
> Mum on the phone while using the hair dryer
> Dead mosquito

I might say, "Dirty dishes! Yes! That's something we all have. So how will you write about your dirty dishes? Do you know yet?"

"Well, it's my job to wash them, and I really hate doing it. Maybe I'll write that dishes get dirty during the night all by themselves. When I wake up, there they are in the sink again."

"Great idea! That's really funny! Maybe they have parties during the night while you and your family are snoring away. I love it! Who's next?"

Give everyone an opportunity to contribute but move quickly. Don't let the conversation drag. The goal now is to build enthusiasm and excitement for the writing assignment!

End the period on a high note and announce that everyone is now going to settle on one way to write about his or her idea and begin work on a poem. You can provide time to write during school or give your students a few nights to work at home.

"Next time," you can say, "we're going to hear some great poems about common things around the house. Who would guess that they would turn into poems!"

Day Four (30–60 minutes)

Sharing the Poems

Today is the big day to share poems. Establish a spot in front of the class for the speaker and explain the rules. There are three: Each student does his or her best job of reading so that everyone can enjoy the poem; the class applauds to show its appreciation for all that good work; and two or three positive, specific comments about each poem are encouraged. You may ask for comments orally or in writing.

A poem written by a third grader is at the right. Several positive, reinforcing comments come to mind.

"I really love your idea," I say, "of a cat that looks like a mat!"

"Your choice of words—barely chase a rat, you sat on her, you can always find her—gives me a wonderful picture of a cat who is so fat she can scarcely waddle across the room to her food dish."

"And the way you have organized your poem, by repeating 'Because she is so fat,' is a powerful, funny reminder of your cat's problem."

Have fun! Consider binding these poems into a collection to keep on display all year. Share them with another class. Talk to your librarian about putting the collection in the library for a time so that other students can enjoy the poetry. You might also consider letting your students take turns bringing the collection home to show their families.

Student Poem

MY FAT CAT
by Emmie Wagner

My cat looks like a mat
Because she is so fat.
One day upon her I sat
Because she is so fat.
She can barely chase a rat
Because she is so fat.
We always know where she's at
Because she is so fat.

Name _____ Date _____

Poetry Page

CATS

by Eleanor Farjeon

Cats sleep
Anywhere,
Any table,
Any chair,
Top of piano,
Window-ledge,
In the middle,
On the edge,
Open drawer,
Empty shoe,
Anybody's
Lap will do,
Fitted in a
Cardboard box,
In the cupboard
With your frocks—
Anywhere!
They don't care!
Cats sleep
Anywhere.

BABY SPIDER

by David L. Harrison

Noiselessly the spider plunges
Like a diver off my door,
A tiny living dot that dangles
Seven feet above the floor.

Bungee-jumping astronaut,
Miniature member of his race,
Letting out his silver cord
He works defenselessly in space.

Disappearing, reappearing,
Lost in shadow, bathed in light,
He slowly inches undetected,
Patient in his daring flight.

The floor at last beneath his feet
He ends his risky episode
And sets out on a new adventure
Down the carpet's nappy road.

LIFE'S NOT FAIR!

by David L. Harrison

I changed the roll
An hour ago
So there'd be plenty there.

I'm telling you
The roll was new,
We even had a spare.

So now I go,
And don't you know,
The roll's completely bare,

I have to yelp
And cry for help!
Life just isn't fair!

Using the Power of Poetry to Teach Language Arts, Social Studies, Science, and More *Scholastic Professional Books*

CHAPTER 3

My Dreams for Tomorrow

Setting Goals for Ourselves and Our Community

Every child must be loved because without love, children will be heartbroken and the earth will be nothing but a sphere with unfeeling people.

–Iris, Grade 6

The qualities that make us human are our ability to think, to set goals, and to dream. This chapter focuses on guiding children to set social and academic goals in the classroom, to reflect on what they value about America, and to consider what elements go into making a successful community. It challenges them to look at the present and the future, and it invites them to think about how they can make a difference in their school, community, and country. This chapter can be easily incorporated into a social studies unit at any grade level.

Using lists, webs, and discussions with family members and classmates, students examine their hopes, goals, and dreams. They then use the power of poetry to help them crystallize their thoughts and express them in carefully crafted pieces.

FROM KATHY'S CLASSROOM

The Dream Jar
Setting Academic and Personal Goals

Focus Lessons:

❧ Poets sometimes write poems that have a message.

❧ Poets sometimes repeat a word or phrase
to make their message or idea clear.

■ ■ ■ ■ ■ ■ ■

Materials Suggested

❧ *The Dream Jar*, by Bonnie Pryor (Morrow Jr. Books, 1996). Poems: "Martin Luther King," by Myra Cohn Livingston; "My Dream Star," by David L. Harrison; "Dreams," by Langston Hughes; and "I Look Around Me," by Alexandra Prater (pages 53–54)

❧ Dream Theme Goal-Setting Sheet (page 55)

❧ Dream Theme Web (page 56)

❧ Our Dream Jar reproducible (page 57)

❧ One large glass or clear plastic jar (to be labeled "Our Dream Jar")

On a practical level, when students set goals for themselves, they accomplish more, as is true of everyone. Whether it's the goal of finishing math homework or learning to play the violin, articulating a wish helps us steer a course toward achieving it. And on a more soulful level, defining one's dreams—and going after their fulfillment—is one of the most precious things we can guide our children to do. Poetry gives children an opportunity to think about their wishes, hopes, and dreams, not only for the school year but for the rest of their lives.

Poet's Note

Here's another case, I think, where poetry becomes the vehicle for teaching one of life's important lessons: how to dream. Most boys and girls will tell us what they want to be when they grow up. In their games, they swerve and roar around in race cars or hide from sharks in hidden grottoes or defend the empire with miniature plastic swords. They try on fantasies of their future as easily as shoes and socks, and they outgrow them even faster. But to really think about what it might take, or how it might feel, to one day become a climber of mountains, a defender of the poor, a teacher of children—that's the stuff of dreams.

At my school, we encourage our students to set goals (with teacher guidance) at least twice a year. My students write their goals, which I share with parents at parent conferences. I make two copies. One is put into the student portfolio, and the other is sent home. Sometimes I have students write their goals on three-by-five-inch cards and tape them to their desks, where they may look at them often. Using this unit at the beginning of the year helps to set high standards for achievement and to develop a community of learners where individual opinions are appreciated and valued.

Day One (60 minutes or less)

Setting the Stage With a Read Aloud

I gather my students in my reading area and show them *The Dream Jar* by Bonnie Pryor. I have all of them look carefully at the cover and I ask them, "What do you think this story is about?" Katie, one of my students, says that she thinks a little girl is saving money for something because there is a jar with coins on the cover of the book. Chase says that he thinks the story took place a long time ago because of the setting and what the little girl is wearing. (The story is about an immigrant family that works together and saves money in order to achieve the dream of owning a store in a better part of New York City.)

As I read the story, we discuss how the entire family contributes to make their dream come true. At first, the little girl can't figure out how she can make a contribution, but finally she begins giving English lessons to some of the people living in her apartment building. The little girl tells her students that when she grows up, she would like to become a teacher. My entire class loves the story.

I share that becoming a teacher has been my dream since I was a small child. Then I ask the class to whisper their dreams to someone sitting near them. After that, some of the class members share their dreams aloud. Ben wants to become a scientist, while Chase wants to become a professional hockey player.

Next, I show them a large plain jar and the reproducible, Our Dream Jar (page 57). I ask my students to think about the dreams and goals that they have for this school year and for the future, then announce that we're going to write down our dreams and put them in our own dream jar. My students want to get to work immediately, but I tell them that they have to wait until tomorrow. I also ask if anyone would be willing to design a label for our dream jar. Amy and McKenna quickly volunteer. Later in the day, they decorate our jar and the results are beautiful. The class loves it!

> **Student Poem**
>
> ### WISH, TOO ...
> *by Chase Komatz*
>
> I, too, wish to see
>   the ocean sparkling in the sun ...
>
> I, too, wish to see
>   the animals jumping here and there ...
>
> I, too, wish to see
>   the rain forest dazzling in the sunlight ...
>
> If we try to make
>   the world a better place,
>   it will happen ...

Day Two   (45 minutes or less)

Brainstorming Ideas

I pass out several poems, and the class puts them into their Poetry, Song, and Rap booklets. We share the poems aloud. I ask them, "Which of the poems is your favorite and why?" They love Mr. Harrison's "My Dream Star." Ben says, "Mr. Harrison wants us to reach for the stars!" They are also very moved by "I Look Around Me". They think that Alexandra has very good word choice. Alee says, "I notice that she repeats 'anything is possible' several times." I respond, "That is an excellent observation, Alee. Many times, writers repeat a word or a phrase in order to emphasize something. These techniques help them express their message clearly."

Next, I ask them to think about dreams that they might have for school, for the community, for the future, and dreams that might make the world a better place. I model, "One dream I have for this school year is to share many beautiful, funny, and exciting poems with you. I also want you to write your own wonderful poems this year. In our class library, I have two shelves of poetry books. During free reading time you might want to select one of these books to read." I pass out the Dream Theme Web (page 56) and ask them to jot down some of their ideas. (The web ideas can be placed in their writers' notebooks or journals.)

Day Three   (30 minutes)

Sharing Ideas

I ask students to get out their dream webs and to share some of their hopes and dreams. McKenna says that she wants to become a professional dancer. She has been taking lessons and performing for several years. Allie says that she wants to become a teacher. After a few more students have shared, I ask them to add ideas to their dream webs. Then I pass out the Our Dream Jar reproducible (page 57). I ask them to look over their web and write down at least three dreams that they have. I invite students to share a few ideas, and then we carefully fold our sheets and place them in Our Dream Jar.

Day Four   (15 minutes)

Teaching the Focus Lesson

I begin by asking students to get out the dream poems and to reread them in small groups or in pairs. I encourage them to have their Dream Theme Webs out and to add to them if they think of something new.

After five or ten minutes of rereading the poems, I ask the class to come over to the easel with the poems. We discuss how poets are often inspired to write poems that have a strong message and notice that sometimes poets repeat a word or phrase in order to emphasize an important idea. Shelby says, "'I Look Around Me' has a strong message and it repeats . . . *anything is possible*." "Wonderful observation, Shelby. And what a powerful message, made even stronger by its repetition. When a poet begins stanzas with the same word or phrase, I like to call it a stanza starter. It's a helpful way to emphasize an important idea. You might want to try using a stanza starter for your dream poems. Let's brainstorm some together now." I write the student suggestions on chart paper. Here's the list one third-grade class came up with:

1. Sometimes I wish . . .   **5.** What good are dreams?
2. If I try . . .   **6.** It is my hope and dream . . .
3. I hope some day . . .   **7.** How do dreams start?
4. I wish . . .

I also mention that poets use the same technique to end a stanza, which I call stanza endings. We take the time to brainstorm as a class and come up with the following:

1. So keep on trying   **4.** Reach for the stars
2. Anything is possible   **5.** Don't ever give up
3. So never give up

I now invite students to begin their own dream poems, using stanza starters or stanza endings, if they choose, to emphasize their message.

Drafting *(15 minutes)*

I write along with them. After ten minutes, I ask them to stop and I share my draft, "It Is My Hope and Dream." When I ask for volunteers to share their poems, everyone clamors for a turn! Matt writes "If We Try," repeating the title throughout the poem. McKenna writes, "I Wish," using the title as a stanza starter. Ben writes a vivid poem about smog, although he doesn't use stanza starters or endings. I am amazed at the wide range of ideas that are shared and the powerful ways in which they are expressed; most students choose to use a stanza starter or ending for emphasis, and the repetition works. I give students time on another day to revise, encouraging them to think about line breaks and white space in connection with repeating phrases. Some samples of their work are on page 52.

Display Ideas

1. Mount the poems on paper pillows and hang them from the ceiling.

2. Students can copy their dreams and goals onto large stars and write captions, such as "Amy's School Goals" or "My Dreams for the Future, by Amy."

3. Mount the poems on blue or white construction paper cut out in the shapes of clouds. Then display them in the hallway or on a bulletin board titled "Our Dreams" or "The Hopes and Dreams for Room 12."

Extension Ideas

1. Read *Miss Rumphius*, by Barbara Cooney. Discuss the goals and dreams that she had in the story.

2. Set a schoolwide goal that can be accomplished during the school year.

3. Become involved in a school or community service project. Each April, to coincide with Earth Day, my community has a Pride Day. On this day, people in my neighborhood clean up trash, plant flowers and trees, work on their walking trails, and help out in other ways.

Student Poems

IF WE TRY
by Matt Sabey

I know if we try
    to save animals
    from becoming extinct
        It will happen . . .

I know if we try
    to have homeless people find homes
    and hungry people have food
        It will happen . . .

I know if we try
    to not have ugly wars
    and fights
        It will happen . . .

I know if we try
    to keep our air clean
    and not have pollution
        It will happen . .

The world can
    become a better place
        only if we try.

SMOG
by Ben Horblit

Cruising down the road I see
A semi barreling on
Belching ugly black smoke
The horrible black cloud
    drifts above us trapped
    in our atmosphere
As it whirls and twirls
    into the sky
    many thoughts in my mind
    float by
I wish the smog
    would vanish
    forever

Poetry Page

I LOOK AROUND ME
by Alexandra Prater, age 8

When I look out the window, I see
fields, flowers, streams, and roads.
But part of what I see is what is
thrown away, to blow and litter.
If we all stop, and think, and help pick up,
.........anything is possible.

When I am going by, I sometimes see
people wrapped up in rags,
huddled on doorsteps.
We want to help but often we are scared,
and it is difficult.
If we all work together,
.........anything is possible.

When I am walking past, I see brilliant colors—
of skin, and hair, and eyes.
But I listen and hear people hating and hurting
all those who are different.
If we look at things with open hearts,
.........anything is possible.

I am only a child, yet I can see so many things.
If everyone can learn to see
with the eyes of a child,
.........anything is possible.

DREAMS
by Langston Hughes

Hold fast to dreams
For if dreams die
Life is a broken-winged bird
That cannot fly.

Hold fast to dreams
For when dreams go
Life is a barren field
Frozen with snow.

Using the Power of Poetry to Teach Language Arts, Social Studies, Science, and More   *Scholastic Professional Books*

Poetry Page

MY DREAM STAR
by David L. Harrison

I see a star
so high
so far above
our planet earth,
our home,
our base
somewhere in space,
and I think and stare
and dare not blink
for fear I'll lose my star,
my special mark—
among a million million marks
in sight—
that finds its way
through trackless space
and endless time
to shine for me
and light my dreams
on earth.

MARTIN LUTHER KING
by Myra Cohn Livingston

Got me a special place
For Martin Luther King.
His picture on the wall
Makes me sing.

I look at it for a long time
And think of some
Real good ways
We will overcome.

Using the Power of Poetry to Teach Language Arts, Social Studies, Science, and More *Scholastic Professional Books*

Name _____ Date _____

Dream Theme Goal-Setting Sheet

Two goals that I have set for this year are:

_____

_____

_____

_____

_____

_____

The reasons that I have set these goals are:

_____

_____

_____

_____

_____

_____

I would like to accomplish these goals by (date): _____

A goal that I have for the future is:

_____

_____

_____

_____

I have set this goal because:

_____

_____

_____

_____

_____

Dream Theme Web

Goals and dreams for this year . . .

_____
_____
_____
_____
_____
_____

Dreams for
my community . . .

_____
_____
_____
_____

Dreams for me
as an adult . . .

_____
_____
_____
_____

Dreams to make the world a better place . . .

_____
_____
_____
_____

Using the Power of Poetry to Teach Language Arts, Social Studies, Science, and More *Scholastic Professional Books*

Our Dream Jar

One dream that I have for this school year is:

_____

_____

_____

_____

_____

_____

_____

_____

One dream that I have for the future is:

_____

_____

_____

_____

_____

_____

_____

_____

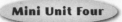

Materials Suggested

- Writers' notebooks
- Poems: "My Valentine" by Clare Miseles; "Hang Out the Flag," by James S. Tippett (page 62)
- One large piece of white butcher paper
- Red and blue marking pens
- Optional: pieces of red, white, and blue construction paper to make the Patriotic Valentines
- Optional: sign entitled "Words From the Heart: What We Love About America"

Mini Unit Four

FROM KATHY'S CLASSROOM

Patriotic Valentines

Recognizing the Strengths of Our Country

Children in the United States are fortunate to live in a country that has educational opportunity and freedom. This mini unit asks children to ponder what they value about the United States and to put their ideas on paper. Your class may finish this unit by designing their own patriotic valentines to go along with their heartfelt poems. This unit may be incorporated into a history unit, a Veterans Day celebration, or Valentine's Day.

Focus Lesson:

Good poets sometimes write poems from their hearts.

· · · · · · ·

Day One (45 minutes)

Setting the Stage

Early in the morning, I ask the students to get out their writers' notebooks. I draw a large heart on the white butcher paper that I've taped on the front board and write "What I Love about America."

I say, "Can anyone share what you love about America? Think about places you've visited, things that you enjoy doing with your family, or symbols that represent America."

Holly says that she loves to see the crashing waves when she visits San Diego. Ryan shares that he loves our Colorado weather with its bright sunshine and azure skies. I carefully record their ideas on the butcher paper, using either a red or blue marking pen.

Once everyone has had a chance to contribute, I say, "Please open up your notebooks to a fresh page, draw a heart, and spend a few minutes jotting down your own ideas about what *you* love about our wonderful country. You may use our brainstormed list to get your thinking started." As the children busily write down their ideas, I circulate, giving words of encouragement.

After a few minutes, I ask if anyone has a new idea that they would be willing to share. Hands shoot up like rockets! Some new ideas are "my caring principal," "Rocky Mountain National Park," and "so many beautiful places to visit."

Day Two (45 minutes)

Teaching the Focus Lesson

"Look at the poems that I've passed out to you. In a moment, we're going to share them aloud," I say. The class reads "My Valentine" and "Hang Out the Flag" out loud (page 62). We then discuss how sometimes poets will select a topic that has deep meaning in their lives and write a poem about it. I call this "writing from your heart," and it's the topic of our focus lesson today.

"Now please get out your notebooks, think about what you love about America—adding any new ideas—and then circle the ideas that are the most meaningful to you, the ones that speak from your heart."

Next, I ask the children to write patriotic poems. I say, "Think about what you feel is special about America. Write with your heart, not your hands."

After students have written their rough drafts, I have them share them in small groups. Then, I confer with each student and encourage my poets to revise based on the feedback they've received. Finally, students edit their poems and write out a fresh copy. I ask students to mount their poems on pieces of red or blue construction paper.

Writing poetry is where my heart is.
–Eve Merriam

Day Three (45 minutes)

Making Patriotic Valentines

(This is an optional activity. Please see photo of a bulletin board idea and some of the completed Patriotic Valentines.)

I place several 12- by 18-inch and 8- by 11-inch pieces of red, white, and blue construction paper at the back of the room and invite students to select one large piece of paper and two smaller pieces, making sure to have one piece of each color.

After all the students have made their choices, I say, "Today I want you to use your imagination and design a large Patriotic Valentine. You may design it any way you'd like, but remember to incorporate all three colors: red, white, and blue."

When the students have finished, I place the poems and valentines on a bulletin board or in the hall. I have also used the completed products as borders for a Washington and Lincoln bulletin board.

No tears for the writer,
no tears for the reader.
–Robert Frost

EXTENSION IDEAS

Community Valentines

Have your students send a valentine to people they know who have contributed something to their community or to people who have served in a branch of the military. Two suggestions follow:

1. After students have completed their patriotic poems and valentines, have the children send them to people who work in hospitals or to personnel who work at police or fire stations.

2. For the past two years, we have had a schoolwide Veterans Day celebration for the men and women who have served our country in the military. The morning begins with a breakfast honoring our veterans. Then there is a schoolwide assembly. Our gym is decked out in a red, white, and blue theme. Our music director leads the students in singing patriotic songs, our principal speaks, and members from each of the branches come up on stage to be honored. Afterward, many of the veterans go into classrooms, share experiences with the students, and answer questions. Next year, my class will give valentines and poems to those who served our country.

In the past, I always taught this unit in February. It seemed to be a perfect fit for celebrating Valentine's Day and Washington's and Lincoln's birthdays.

But 2001 was different. I decided I would start the year out by asking my class for the reasons why they loved America. It was the beginning of September. I drew a heart on a large piece of butcher paper and in the heart I wrote "What I Love About America."

I asked the children to brainstorm ideas in their journal. After a few minutes I said, "Now I'm going to put some of your ideas on the butcher paper." Ideas flow quickly—rushing streams, sunshine, crashing ocean waves, hiking in the cool mountains, fresh water, plenty of food.

I left the butcher paper up on the front board. I told my class that in a few days we would return to the project and they would crystallize their ideas into patriotic poems.

Then came September 11. When we returned to brainstorming and adding ideas to the butcher paper, the majestic mountains and crashing waves vanished. They were replaced by soaring eagles, American flags, the Statue of Liberty, brave firefighters and police officers. The impact of 9/11 had redirected their ideas about what they love about America.

The poems that follow were not written with my students' hands. They were written from their hearts.

RED, WHITE, AND BLUE
by Genna Blanton

The flag of America
Will stand to conquer
Horrible days

And while we wait
Our government
Keeps terrorists away

My family is important to me
All my wishes for freedom come from my heart
My home is America and
I love liberty

The eagle will fly
Over Lady Liberty in peace
The eagle is the symbol of peace
in a silent kind of way
The eagle will soar from
New York to LA spreading its
Peace power

Our Lady will stand in a noiseless
greeting to our new immigrants
from near and far
Our Lady stands for freedom

I thank our Father for all I know
And I pray each night and day
so my family and I will be
safe morning, afternoon, and night

Freedom is a most valuable
possession of all
I will help anyone who has
lost their home
because it is my honor
to keep many people protected
in my country

LIBERTY LAND
by Ryan Camp

Our lady,
the Statue of Liberty
that still stands for freedom.

Our courageous
firefighters, who risk their
lives to save others
because they care.

I salute all Americans,
that help people in so
many ways
each day.

Our God,
that protects us and
gives us hope for
America

Our military
that defends our
country and protects us
and gives us hope
for America

Our president
that makes the right
decisions for America

Our freedom
to believe whatever
we want.

God Bless America

LUCKY
by Kate Baughn

We are lucky
don't you think?

We have freedom
we have books

We have school
and love

Parents, houses and
so much more

America, America
What a wonderful
place to be

America, America
God bless us and thee

We have done great
things, and we won't stop

Poetry Page

MY VALENTINE
by Clare Miseles

I made a valentine,
So different and new.
The heart isn't red,
But red, white and blue.

It's real patriotic
And real loving, too.
I almost forgot;
I made it for you.

HANG OUT THE FLAG
by James S. Tippett

This is Flag Day.
Hang out the flags;
Watch them rise with the
breeze
And droop when it sags.
Hang them from short poles;
Hang them from long.
See their bright colors
Shimmering strong,
Drifting along.

Flags mean our Homeland,
Country we love.
Let them sparkle in sunshine
Proudly above,
Showing our love.

CHAPTER 4

Pieces of the Puzzle

Exploring Science

> Poetry brings sound and sense together in words and lines, ordering them on the page in such a way that both the writer and reader get a different view of life.
>
> –Donald Graves

From the time children are very young, they observe, explore, question, and try to see where they fit into their family, their school, the world. Whether looking through a telescope, doing research on a scientific topic, or putting together pattern blocks, they are gradually able to put some of the pieces in place.

This unit challenges children to be careful observers, collectors, researchers, and questioners when studying math and science. Using the powers of poetry, personification, and pondering, we then ask the children to take their information and write. By writing, they learn to ask questions and find answers along the way.

FROM KATHY'S CLASSROOM

Solar System symphony

Exploring the Planets

> Writing should be discovery, not something that you already know.
>
> –Georgia Heard

Poet's Note

Who has not gazed with wonder into the starry night? I remember my fascination in third grade with the mysterious ways that stars and whole galaxies were said to move in different directions at the same time. The speeds of their flights through the vastness of space left me with far more questions than answers.

No one thought to suggest that I could write about my questions, my awe, my wonder. Yet nothing seems more natural. After all, writers love to write about subjects that fascinate them. And being curious about space is one of our most universal human experiences.

One child might pick up a rock, pretend it is a piece of meteorite, and write about its incredible journey of billions of years and trillions of miles to reach us here on our tiny planet. Someone else might rely on his or her imagination to take a personal trip among the planets or venture even farther to reach the stars themselves. Other young writers may be content to simply ponder the night sky, as I once did, and marvel at the majesty of it all.

This strategy offers many advantages. It gives young writers the largest tablet of all on which to write their impressions. It encourages them to want to know more about their subject. It leads inevitably to math problems that stretch the imagination and leave indelible impressions about our relative size in a mighty universe. So whether we're teaching math, science, writing, or a general appreciation for nature's breathtaking scope and beauty, space is the place!

As any good teacher knows, the secret of success is advanced planning. Before beginning this unit, I put up a solar system bulletin board, which has factual information as well as visual appeal.

Another key to success is stocking my class with books! I make a quick trip to the local library and then visit our well-stocked school library. In both places, I am able to gather a wide variety of nonfiction solar system books, as well as a selection of fictional literature. The space books are placed throughout my classroom: on top of the bookcase, on bookshelves, and in plastic tubs. (See page 68 for titles.) Lastly, I order space videos and plan a field trip to the Denver Museum of Nature and Science.

Focus Lessons:

ℰ Good writers vary the beginnings of their lines.

ℰ Good writers incorporate strong verbs into their poems.

ℰ Good writers sometimes write poetry from a first person perspective ("I").

ℰ Good writers sometimes incorporate factual information into their poems.

ℰ Good writers sometimes incorporate elements found on a self-assessment checklist.

■ ■ ■ ■ ■ ■ ■

Day One (60 minutes or less)

Setting the Stage

Space—just say the word and eyes light up! With one word you've thrown out the bait and they're ready to take the hook.

I have my students bring their clipboards and a pencil to the reading area, and after they settle down I say, "For the next several weeks, our class will be studying space. During this time you will be seeing videos, going on a field trip to the Denver Museum of Nature and Science, doing research on a planet of your choice, reading space books, and searching for information about your planet in books, magazines, and on the Internet. You will also hear a guest speaker and, perhaps, you might even begin thinking about a career that is related to space."

"Can I study about Mars?" asks Corinne excitedly.

"We are going to wait until we've studied the solar system for a few days before anyone selects a planet," I reply.

"Now I'm going to pass out multicolored sticky notes," I say. "On them, I would like each of you to write down something about the solar system that

Materials Suggested

ℰ A bulletin board that shows the solar system

ℰ Various nonfiction books about the solar system

ℰ Assorted videos and movies about the solar system

ℰ Notes on Speakers, Lectures, Videos, and Movies reproducible (page 73)

ℰ Sticky notes

ℰ Three-prong pocketed folders

ℰ 10 to 15 sheets of lined paper

ℰ One or two packs of 5-by-8-inch index cards

ℰ Large paper cups

ℰ *The New York Public Library Kid's Guide to Research*, by Deborah Heiligman (Scholastic Inc., 1998; optional)

ℰ *Holst-The Planets-* CD, (Chandos Records, Ltd., 1998)

ℰ *The Magic School Bus: Lost in the Solar System*, by Joanna Cole (Scholastic Inc., 1990)

ℰ Poem: "I Am the Sun" by David Harrison (page 71)

ℰ Student poems inspired by this lesson (pages 67, 69, and 70)

ℰ Self-Assessment Checklist (page 72)

you've wondered about or a question that you have about space. Remember to write your name on the sticky note. In a few minutes we're going to share our ideas and place them on the large piece of blue butcher paper." Before school, I have placed a piece of butcher paper on our front board and entitled it, "The Solar System: Questions We Have and Things That We Wonder About."

"Who has something that they would like to share?" I ask.

Every hand in the room shoots up. "How many planets have moons?" asks Emily. "How hot does the sun get?" asks Greg. "I wonder if anyone will ever live on Mars," Connor adds.

After all of the students make a contribution, they put their questions on our front board. The butcher paper quickly becomes colorful and the students are excited!! "As you think of a new question, please write it on a sticky note and add it to the butcher paper." The butcher paper stays up during the entire unit. I periodically have the class revisit it to share new ideas and questions that are added.

During the next few minutes, I ask the students to get out their three-prong pocketed folders. I pass out planet informational sheets and ask the students to place them in their folders. After that, they put 10 to 15 sheets of lined paper in their folders. The lined paper will be used later for taking notes. Lastly, they write their names on their folder cover and proceed to turn them into works of art using crayons and marking pens.

Weeks One to Two (approximately 60 minutes each day for one week)

Building a Strong Knowledge Base Through Read Alouds and Partner Reading

"Please come over to the reading area," I say. "Today we are going to begin reading a book about space. But before we begin reading it, I would like you to preview it with a friend. I want you to be 'book detectives.' When you go to your seats, I want each of you to get out a piece of paper and jot down *everything* that you notice about the book." I point to the cover and say, "I notice there is a bus flying in space that is decorated with planets and stars and that there are children in the bus." I quickly jot this idea on my easel. "It is a fictional book that has a great deal of factual information embedded in it." I pass out The Magic School Bus book *Lost in the Solar System* to everyone and tell them to get to work with their partner.

After about five minutes I say, "Stop!" Then I go to the overhead and ask, "What did you discover?" As students share ideas, I jot them on the overhead and say, "You may steal ideas and add them to your list." The children make many wonderful observations.

The first day I usually share part of the Big Book of *Lost in the Solar System*. Then as a class, we share two to three things that were learned, and I jot their ideas on the easel. For the next few days, I ask the children to read their *Lost in the Solar System* book, either independently or with a buddy. In their folder each day, they write about what they learned, discovered, or found interesting.

During the next few days, in addition to reading the Magic School Bus book, I set aside time for watching videos. Before we begin to watch the first video, I pass out the Notes on Speakers, Lectures, Videos, and Movies reproducible (page 73) to each child. I say, "In the next week or two, you will be taking notes on a variety of videos that will teach you about the facts and mysteries of our universe." I place a copy of the note taking reproducible on the overhead and say, "The main idea of this video is . . . . Please copy this information carefully. As you watch the video, please jot down at least three facts that you learn and then list what you found to be the most interesting part."

When the first video ends, I again turn on the overhead and ask the students what they learned. I then write three facts on the overhead that they have shared. As they are writing their facts, I walk around the room to monitor them and see if anyone needs assistance.

"Taking notes is a skill that you will use the rest of your lives. Please store your notes in your space folder. Great job with your note taking!"

Week Two (45–60 minutes per day)

Selecting Planets: Reading, Writing, and Research

I begin by announcing, "During the past two weeks, you've been learning about our universe. Today is the day that you will select a planet, the moon, or the sun to study. I don't want more than two students studying the same planet so please have a second one in mind." I get out my clipboard with a class list attached and ask each child to make a selection. By now they are chomping at the bit and can't wait to get started!

Once everyone has made a selection, we move on to the research cards. I ask my trusty paper monitors to pass out five index cards and a large paper clip to each class member. When everyone has their cards and paper clips, I go to the overhead and write "Research Card Information." Then I say, "Please write one of the following questions at the top of each card."

1. How did my planet get its name? Does it have any nicknames?

2. What is unique or special about my planet?

3. Interesting facts and physical characteristics of my planet

4. How does my planet move?

5. References (where I found my information)

"Please keep these cards in your pocketed folder," I say. "During the next few

---

Student Poem

I AM
by Ben Coyle

I am Mars, the Roman god of war
Home to the most vast volcano of all,
       Olympus Mons
My atmosphere is mostly carbon dioxide
I spin like a huge UFO
I am 248,000,000 miles away from Earth
I am the fourth planet from the Sun
Did you know they think
       I might have water on me?
I have two bumpy moons on me
       named Demos and Phobus
All the time,
 I have enormous swirling duststorms
I AM THE RED PLANET, MARS

days, you will find answers to your questions by reading books and doing searches on the Internet. I would like you to explore at least three sources, so you'll have three or more references. Later in this unit, you will use your information to develop a first person narrative poem. You will become your planet!"

The next few days are a flurry of activity. My class is on a fact finding mission. Every spare moment is spent reading books about their planet, looking up information in encyclopedias, searching the Internet, and compiling the information on their cards.

BOOK LINKS

Solar System

The Mystery of Mars by Sally Ride and Tam O'Shaughnessy (Crown, 1999)

The Planets—Neighbors in Space, by Jeanne Bendick (Milbrook Press, 1991)

Postcards From Pluto, by Loreen Leedy (Holiday House, 1993)

Questions and Answers— Stars and Planets, by Robin Kerrod (Kingfisher, 2002)

Solar System, by Gregory Vogt (Scholastic Inc., 2001)

Venus by Seymour Simon (Morrow Jr., 1992)

Focus Lesson (*(30–45 minutes)*

First Person Narrative and Other Discoveries

After several days of research, I begin class by asking for silence and saying, "Who can share with the class an example of a first person narrative poem?" For once, not one person in my enthusiastic class raises a hand.

"Well, you are in luck! I just happen to have several examples of this form of poetry." I pass out copies of the poems (page 71) and place one poem at a time on the overhead. We read each one aloud. After David Harrison's "I Am the Sun" poem and the student-authored poems are shared, I ask each child to put the poems in their space folders. "Now in your groups, I would like you to discuss what you think is unique or special about these poems."

After a few minutes, I ask the class what they have discovered. Chase notices that the poems begin with "I am." Genna says that the poets include how the planets move. She adds that the poets use strong verbs. Another child says that they vary the beginnings of the lines.

"All of those things are excellent observations but what makes these poems first person narratives is that the poet becomes the planet and uses 'I' in the poem."

"Look at these poems now and then. They might help you as you begin writing your own space poems." At this point, I pass out the Self-Assessment Checklist on page 72 so students know what to include in their poems.

Another Day (*(30–45 minutes)*

Drafting the Poems

I begin by saying, "You have worked so hard on your research cards. Please get them out and look them over. They will be invaluable to you today. Think about what is unique or special about your planet. Think about how it moves. Think about how you can become your planet. Today, just get some of your thoughts down on paper. When I turn on *The Planets* by Holst, I want you to listen to the music carefully and write." (The idea of incorporating this CD was shared with me by my good friend Honey Goldberg.) As the sound of the music begins to float across my room, something magical begins. The children are inspired, and their pencils move. Their poems begin to take shape.

After 15 to 20 minutes, I ask them to stop writing and share their drafts with a buddy. I pass out several sticky notes to each child and say, "On your first note, write one thing that you thought was powerful about your classmate's poem, and on your second note write one suggestion that you think might improve the poem. Give the notes to your classmate after he or she has finished sharing."

Another Day (30–45 minutes)

Revising the Poems

"What does revision mean?" I ask. "It means to look at something carefully. Today before you begin to write, I want you to reread your poem and look at the sticky notes that were given to you by your classmates. Remember, when you revise, think about what makes a poem powerful. Ask yourself questions from the checklist: Do I have a great beginning? Do I show, not tell, how I move in the universe? Have I included interesting information? Remember that you might want to cross things out, add on, or change the order of your lines. Good luck, poets! Start revising!"

After 15 or 20 minutes, I once more have them pair up with a buddy, and take turns noting strong points and areas for possible further revision. As always, the poet can choose whether or not to incorporate the suggestions into his or her poem.

The Next Day (30–45 minutes)

Self-Assessment Checklist Focus Lesson

First thing in the morning I say to my students, "You have worked so hard on your poetry drafts. Today I want you to use the checklist to evaluate your poem. As you read your poem, notice whether or not you have incorporated the suggestions into your poem. If you have, please put a check in the category."

After they have completed their checklists, they sign up to have their poems edited one more time with me.

* Feel free to adapt this list to meet your needs. If you teach fragile learners, just have them incorporate two or three of the elements. If you want to challenge a very able poet, add one or two new categories.

> **Student Poem**
>
> **I AM**
> by Ben Klass
>
> I am Neptune
> I am named after the Roman god of the sea
> John Couch Adams, a college professor, found me
> I'm a jovian planet
>   located far away from the Sun
> I have the fastest moving clouds
>   in the solar system
> My clouds consist of frozen methane
> My five rings orbit up
>   and down around me
> You rarely see me in the sky
> A huge dark spot
>   like a swirling fast cyclone
>   is on my clouds
> I wonder if man will ever set foot on me?
>   I AM NEPTUNE

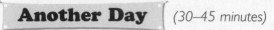

Another Day (30–45 minutes)

Preparing the Final Draft

The class is now ready to type or write their final drafts. After their final drafts have been completed, the poems can be mounted on blue or black construction paper, and decorated with stars, comets, or spaceships using watercolors or crayons. They then can be displayed on a bulletin board entitled, "Our Poetry Is Out of This World!"

Student Poem

I AM

by Jessica Strunk

I am Jupiter
The Roman king of the planets
I spin ever so quickly
I swirl like the wind
My atmosphere is mainly hydrogen gas
Am I really 482,546,000 miles away from the sun?
My big red eye can swallow two earths
My four largest moons are Europa, Ganymade, Io, and Callisto
I am a vast planet
        I AM JUPITER!

Extension and Display Activities

1. Silhouette Outer Space Scenes: Have the students wet a large piece of white construction paper and then splatter it with "cool" shades (blue, green, purple) of watercolors. Let the splattered paper dry. Have students cut out black silhouettes of spaceships, stars, and planets, then glue the silhouettes onto the paper. Students may want to glue their poems onto the completed art project.

2. Vincent van Gogh "Starry Night" Art Project: Discuss that Van Gogh was a Dutch Expressionist who used bold colors to express his moods and emotions. Share the book *Visiting Vincent van Gogh* (Prestel, 1997) or a print of "Starry Night." This painting shows movement and feeling through his use of color and brushstrokes.

Then, pass out black construction paper and tempera paint. Have the students make swirling outer space scenes using the tempera paint. Allow the paintings to dry, then glue on glitter for an even more dramatic effect.

3. Take a field trip to your local natural history museum and explore the space exhibits. Be certain to have the students take notes while they are there!

4. Invite guest speakers to share current information and the latest research with your students.

5. Invite guest speakers to discuss possible space careers, such as becoming an aeronautical engineer, an astronomer, or an astronaut.

6. Celebrate Space Day as a school or within your own classroom. It is the first Thursday in May. Last year, on Space Day, our school was fortunate enough to have a former astronaut share his experiences with us.

7. Space Riddles—Who Am I? Have the children write three clues about something in the solar system on a piece of paper and then ask, "Who am I?"

Poetry Page

I AM THE SUN
by David L. Harrison

I am the Sun,
the star,
great sphere of gas,
mother to a bustling galaxy.

My nine handsome planets
swing around me
like balls on strings
saved by the embrace
of my gravity
from spinning off forever,
homeless in space.

My heat warms their faces,
even impish Pluto and Neptune
who keep switching places
and taking their sweet time
getting their circling done.

I'm constantly upset!
My nuclear stomach
40 million degrees hot
belches gas
that would scorch your moon
and the wind of my breath
carries even farther
to the cold dark reaches
of my realm.

At half a million miles an hour
I hurtle through the universe,
pick a path through the Milky Way,
and pass among the stars
on a journey to a future
too distant to know.

But this I do know—
wherever my journeys lead,
no matter how far,
my brood will be with me.
I am their Sun,
their star.

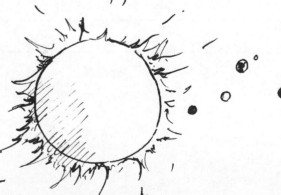

Self-Assessment Checklist

The planet, moon, or star that I selected was _____ .

My poem has the following elements:

	Yes	Partly	No
1. I wrote a first person narrative poem. It includes the word "I" in it.			
2. I varied the beginnings of several of the lines in my poem.			
3. I included at least three or four facts about my planet.			
4. I shared how my planet was named.			
5. I included words/phrases that describe what my planet looks like.			
6. I included two or more strong verbs that tell how my planet moves.			

I think my poem is (circle one choice)

well done, average, or in need of improvement because _____

_____

_____

Using the Power of Poetry to Teach Language Arts, Social Studies, Science, and More *Scholastic Professional Books*

Name _____ Date _____

Notes on Speakers, Lectures, Videos, and Movies

The main idea was _____

_____

_____

_____

_____

Fact #1 _____

_____

_____

_____

Fact #2 _____

_____

_____

_____

Fact #3 _____

_____

_____

_____

One thing that I found to be especially interesting was _____

_____

_____

_____

Materials Suggested

- Board or easel
- Writers' Notebooks
- Poems: "Travel Plans" by Bobbi Katz; "We Wonder," by David L. Harrison (page 77)

Mini Unit Five

FROM DAVID'S TRAVELS

What We Wonder About Our Wonderful World

Asking Questions, Finding Answers

The ability to wonder is one of the most distinguishing and essential privileges of being human. Children wonder about everything. They ask questions. They learn. As adults, entangled in life's embrace like wrestlers in the ring, we can't get a hand free to call "time out;" there never seems time enough to pause or to wonder.

Give children a chance, and they'll drive you wild with questions. "I wonder what makes the ocean salty." "What makes sugar sweet?" "I wonder why cows eat grass." But behind their questions are active minds in hot pursuit of knowledge of all kinds. Several years ago I asked some classes of fourth and fifth graders to send me lists of the things they wondered about. Their teachers collected 1,500 questions, and I spent the following two years answering as many as possible. The project became a book.

Asking questions, wondering about things, is part of growing up. And taking advantage of children's need to know is what makes this exercise fun.

Focus Lesson:

Good writers wonder.

·······

Day One (15 minutes)

Setting the Stage

Read Bobbi Katz's poem, "Travel Plans" (page 77). It's a great way to start a conversation about all the things we might like to do, things we are curious about and wish we could see or taste or feel or hear or experience for ourselves.

"Did you know," you might tell your students, "that many books have been written about the things people wonder about? Being curious about something is a great way to start writing. What do you wonder about? Just for fun, let's start a list on the board."

Once your students begin, it's hard to stop. But keep this first session brief. Just note a few of their questions on the board, then stop and admire their curiosity. Here is a partial list compiled by a class of fourth graders.

How did the world begin?

How are people made?

How do oceans form?

Who invented books?

How hot is it in the middle of the earth?

Why did violence start?

Could the dinosaurs return?

How many sorts of insects are there?

How many turtles are there?

What are spiderwebs made of?

Why is space black?

How many hairs do we have?

How many cells do our bodies have?

How can a bull shark live in salt and fresh waters?

"There is no telling how many things you kids could think of!" you might brag. "I have an idea. For next time, make a list in your writer's notebook of the things you wonder about. Let's find out how many questions you have. How many do you think there will be altogether? I say you'll have more than a hundred!" (Make a list on the board of students' names and their guesses.)

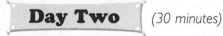 **Day Two**   (30 minutes)

Drafting Poems

Stand at the board and ask everyone to count the number of things on their lists. Add the numbers on the board and congratulate everyone for doing such a good job. See who came closest to guessing the correct number.

"Now that we have all these wonderful lists," you say, "let's see if we can turn some of your ideas into a poem. Here's an example to help get us started."

Read the poem "We Wonder" (page 77) and discuss how the poet used a list just like theirs and turned it into a poem.

Now you can facilitate the writing of a list poem by asking each student to provide one thing that he or she wonders about.

A writer should cultivate only what naturally absorbs his fancy, whether it be freedom or cinch bugs.

–E.B. White

Hint: The first time through, don't worry about making a poem. Just get the list on the board. Stand back and review what your class has created. Do you spot themes (space, animals, school, family, and so forth) that suggest natural arrangements into stanzas or groupings? Move things around and concentrate on one category (stanza) at a time. It may help your young poets to start feeling the flow of their emerging poem if you begin most of the lines with something catchy like "We wonder," "We wish we knew," "Why oh why," or "Does anyone know?" For other helpful ideas to organize your poem, refer back to the lesson on stanza starters and stanza endings (pages 50–51).

Leave your final version of the poem on the board and ask everyone to copy it into their writer's notebook.

"Now," you announce, "I want to see what sort of list poem you can write on your own! You have all these ideas to work with. Let's find out what happens when you write poems about the things you wonder about. We'll share some of them next time."

Day Three (30 minutes)

Sharing the Poems

Ask for volunteers to read their "wonder poems" to the class. When you finish listening, and applauding, decide what to do with so many terrific creations. If you see several topics of interest, consider displaying them under clip art or designs that depict the subject area: space, nature, geography, and history.

> It may be those who do most, dream most.
> —Stephen Leacock

Name _____ Date _____

Poetry Page

TRAVEL PLANS
by Bobbi Katz

If you could go anywhere, where would you go?
Deep in the jungle? Deep in the snow?
Deep in the ocean to talk to a fish?
If you could go anywhere that you could wish

If I could go anywhere, here's what I'd do:
I'd pop in the pouch of a kind kangaroo.
I'd travel around for as long as I please,
And learn to say "thank you" in Kangarooese.

I'd make myself little and then I would see
The part of a flower that interests a bee,
The way the world looks from the tail of a kite,
The way the birds sleep in their nests in the night.

I'd go through the hole in a needle, like thread.
I'd spin like a top on the point of my head.
I'd skate on an ice cube. I'd swim in a glass.
I'd talk to a grasshopper, if any should pass.

And when I got tired of being so small,
I'd ABRACADABRA myself to be tall!
I'd step over oceans. I'd step over seas.
I'd cause a few shipwrecks, if I had to sneeze.

I'd pet a giraffe on the top of his head.
I'd find out for sure, if the North Pole was red.
And when I had seen all that I want to see,
I hope I'd know how to turn back into me.

WE WONDER
by David L. Harrison

We wonder what makes water wet,
We wonder why we need a skin,
We wonder why our teeth fall out
If more are going to grow back in.

Who made candy taste so good
When no one lets us have enough?
Why is Mother's face so smooth
But Daddy's face can be so rough?

We wonder if a turtle itches,
Why a robin swallows worms,
If a skunk can tell he smells,
If a germ gets sick from germs.

We wonder if a fox is smart,
We wonder if a chicken's dumb,
We wonder why a cow eats grass,
We wonder why we have a thumb.

We wonder what puts light in lightning,
What puts all the noise in thunder.
The world is full of things to know,
To think about and wonder!

Using the Power of Poetry to Teach Language Arts, Social Studies, Science, and More · Scholastic Professional Books

CHAPTER 5

Math Senses

Seeing Numbers and Patterns in Daily Life

> Poetry teaches
> 'life' lessons.
> –Georgia Heard

*L*ike it or not, we live in a mathematical world. As teachers, we need to emphasize math concepts, such as computation, problem solving, and logical reasoning, on a daily basis. Math skills are needed throughout life, so if we can make math exciting and interesting, we have a better chance of having our students learn these essential skills.

This unit is filled with quick activities that help children find where numbers and patterns are lurking. The unit is divided into sections on time, numbers, and geometric shapes. Each section includes a focus lesson, materials needed, and lesson plans. Some sections include model and student written poems.

I hope that you have fun with this unit. Let's get started before we run out of time!

FROM KATHY'S CLASSROOM

Time

Each day, I devote 45 minutes or more to teaching math. Whenever possible, I integrate math concepts into the social studies or science unit that I'm teaching. For instance, in a solar system unit, I might ask, "How far is Venus from the Earth?" or "How much farther is Saturn from the Sun than Mars?"

The following activities provide an excellent way to build enthusiasm and motivation for learning mathematical concepts by inviting students to become active participants. I have found that by asking my students to jot their observations in their math logs, I am encouraging them to think creatively and divergently. What's more, by sharing the ideas with their classmates, they are increasing their knowledge base. Everyone benefits, including the teacher!

Focus Lessons:

📧 Good writers sometimes collect words and phrases about a topic.

📧 They use their lists as a springboard for writing.

■ ■ ■ ■ ■ ■ ■

Day One (30 minutes)

Setting the Stage

It is late March, the week before spring break. The weather is gloomy and so is the mood of my class. I know that I have to do something that will spark their interest and bring sunshine into my classroom once more.

"Get out your notebooks and a pencil. And line up," I say.

"What are we doing?" asks Brett.

"You'll see."

Our first stop is the cafeteria. "Please write 'time' on the top of your paper," I say. As we enter the kitchen, I ask the cooks to tell us about all the ways they use time. They tell us that they use it when they are baking things, to know when the fourth grade should be served lunch, to know

Materials Suggested

📧 Math logs or writers' notebooks

📧 Poems: "Ten Minutes Till the Bus," by David L. Harrison; "Time Passes," by Ilo Orleans; "There Isn't Time," by Eleanor Farjeon (page 82)

how long it takes for a dishwashing cycle to be completed. My students write as fast as they can!

Our next stop is the gym. This time we interview our physical education coach. Their "time" lists get longer.

From there, it is on to the office, where our helpful secretaries share more time ideas. Appointments that our principal needs to keep, times for faculty meetings, committee meeting times, and field trips to be scheduled are just a few of the ideas they mention. My class is wildly taking notes as each new idea is introduced. We thank our secretaries and return to our classroom.

Math is over for the day, but for homework I ask students to think about all the different ways that people use time in their everyday lives.

The class is no longer gloomy. They are enthusiastic and engaged!

Day Two (30–45 minutes)

Teaching the Focus Lesson and Drafting the Poems

The next morning I begin the lesson by passing out several poems about time (page 82). As each poem is shared, I ask the class what is interesting or special about the poem.

"My favorite is 'Ten Minutes Till the Bus,' Kate says. "I like it because it's funny and some kids don't like to rush in the morning."

Hayden says, "'There Isn't Time' has an important message. We have to decide what is important in our lives and try to spend time doing it!"

I say, "I love your observations. These poets all chose time as their theme. Today we are going to discuss how writers, especially poets, sometimes collect words and phrases about a topic they're interested in. They use their lists as a springboard for writing. I bet some of these poets had words about time written in their notebooks before they began writing."

"Get out your writers' notebooks or a piece of paper and brainstorm words or phrases that have to do with time of have the word *time* in them."

On the overhead, I write "Time" and model a few ideas for the class: take time to smell the roses, a stopwatch, tick tock, and so on.

I say, "Now it is your turn. You have ten minutes. Write fast! Look around the room and use your marvelous minds! Go!"

After ten minutes, I say, "Stop! Who would like to share?"

Everyone wants to share! As I call on students, I add their ideas to the overhead and say, "You may 'steal' ideas and add them to your lists."

Here is a list of some of their ideas:

- time machine
- timed tests
- nighttime, daytime, noontime
- timer
- reading time
- leisure time
- timing is everything

- *Time for Kids* magazine
- clock in, clock out
- free time
- time capsule
- watches, clocks
- time schedule
- flight time

I say, "Please look over your lists. Find one or two ideas that are interesting or intriguing to you. Circle that idea or those ideas."

After a minute or two, I ask students to get out a fresh piece of paper and write their chosen time word at the top. "Now take the topic and write a poem about it. Remember this is a rough draft. Just get your ideas on your paper." I join in. We all write without stopping for the next 10 or 15 minutes. The rough draft results are amazing. Here are two samples:

Student Poems

NIGHT TIME
by Kelly Condon

Every evening
     before midnight
I go outside and see
     the beautiful moon shining
          over me
It shines so brightly
     with the stars so near
It makes it seem
     I have nothing to fear.

FREE TIME
by Holly Bishop

After school
     it is free time!
I could do Nintendo or
     I could do nap time
All that really matters
     is that it is free time.

 **Day Three** (*30–45 minutes*)

Sharing and Polishing

The third day I have my students share in small groups. They give one another advice and then sign up for final polishing with me. I share with them that I am awestruck by their writing. "What fantastic poets you are!"

The completed poems are mounted on clocks and displayed on a bulletin board entitled "All About Time."

Poetry Page

TEN MINUTES TILL THE BUS
By David L. Harrison

Ten whole minutes
Till the bus,
Scads of time,
What's the fuss?
Two to dress,
One to flush,
Two to eat,
One to brush,
That leaves four
To catch the bus,
Scads of time,
What's the fuss?

THERE ISN'T TIME
By Eleanor Farjeon

There isn't time, there isn't time
To do the things I want to do,
With all the mountain-tops to climb,
And all the woods to wander through,
And all the seas to sail upon,
And everywhere there is to go,
and all the people, every one
Who lives upon the earth, to know.
There's only time, there's only time
To know a few, and do a few,
And then sit down and make a rhyme
About the rest I want to do.

TIME PASSES
By Ilo Orleans

Sixty seconds
Pass in a minute.
Sixty minutes
Pass in an hour.
Twenty-four hours
Pass in a day—
And that's how TIME
Keeps passing away

Using the Power of Poetry to Teach Language Arts, Social Studies, Science, and More   Scholastic Professional Books

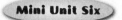
FROM KATHY'S CLASSROOM

Numbers

Focus Lesson:

Good writers make careful observations and incorporate
some of the ideas into their poems

• • • • • • •

Day One (45 minutes)

Setting the Stage

I begin this lesson by saying, "Please come over to the reading area, sit down, and close your eyes."

"Why are you having us close our eyes?" questions Rachel.

I say, "Everyone keep your eyes closed. Rachel, you will find out your answer very soon. Today I'm going to put a 'math curse' on each one of you."

I pause for a few seconds, then say, "Now you may open your eyes."

As they open their eyes, I begin to share Jon Scieszka's *Math Curse*. I have them look at the cover and predict what the book is about. Emily thinks it's about a boy who is surrounded by numbers and he can't get away from them.

I say, "As I read the story, listen carefully and observe the illustrations carefully, too."

After I've read two or three pages, I ask them to "buddy share" special math ideas that they heard as I read or special things that they observed in the illustrations.

I finish reading the story and then say, "Go quickly to your seats and get out your notebooks. Write 'Math Curse' at the top. Then list all the ways that math and numbers were used in the story."

After about ten minutes, we stop and share.

I close the lesson by passing out the Numbers Please! reproducible (page 87) and saying, "Tonight you have a math curse. I want you to take some time tonight to look closely at your surroundings—at home, at school, on the bus—and pay attention to all the ways you notice numbers being used. Record what you notice on this sheet. Be sure to bring it back tomorrow!"

Materials Suggested

- Numbers Please! reproducible (page 87) or writers' notebooks
- *Math Curse*, by Jon Scieszka (Viking, 1995)
- Poems: "Take a Number," by Mary O'Neil; "Marvelous Math," by Rebecca Kai Dotlich; "Math Advice" by David L. Harrison (page 86)

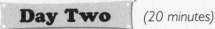

Day Two (20 minutes)

Brainstorming Ideas

"How many of you did your homework?" I ask as they arrive for class.

Everyone has completed the assignment and some students have surprised me by filling in the back side.

"Please get your sheets out and share some of your ideas with me. You may want to add some ideas to your list as we go along."

I jot their ideas on the overhead. Here is a partial list of their discoveries:

- Roman numbers
- a person's age
- street addresses
- a Social Security number
- dice

- a checkbook
- money
- license plates
- the speedometer
- fractions

- sports uniforms
- dates on calendars
- bus numbers
- flight numbers

The list goes on and on. I end the lesson by saying, "Save your sheets in your desk."

Day Three (45 minutes)

Teaching the Focus Lesson and Drafting the Poems

I begin by saying "We've spent some time carefully observing numbers and how they're used in everyday life. Today our writing focus lesson is *Good writers make careful observations and incorporate some of the ideas into their poems.* Can you guess what we are going to do? But first let's look at a few poems about numbers and math and see what some other writers have observed about numbers." I place "Marvelous Math" (page 86) on the overhead and give each student a copy. We share the poem aloud and then I ask, "What do you notice about the poem?"

Connor says, "The poem asks questions, and the answers are all numbers."

"That's right!"

Next I put "Take a Number" (page 86) on the overhead and once again we read it aloud.

This time I ask the children to get into groups of two or three and jot their observations right on the copy of the poem.

I finish the poem share by putting David Harrison's "Math Advice" (page 86) on the overhead and asking the students to join me in reading the poem aloud. Then I ask them what they notice about Mr. Harrison's poem. They notice that it is about numbers, that it has rhythm to it, and that it has a funny ending.

"Now I'd like you to take out your Numbers Please! homework sheet where you recorded your observations of numbers. Today you are going to write your own numbers poem, based on your observations. Let's get writing!"

I write, too. After 15 to 20 minutes, we stop writing and the children put their number drafts away.

Day Four *(30–45 minutes)*

Revising, Editing, and Final Drafts

"Today look at your poem with 'new eyes.' Revise by adding on, crossing out, and changing words. When you feel you have a finished product, self-edit and then sign up for final editing with me."

I am amazed how most of my students have incorporated rhythm into their poems. It seems magical to me.

Here are examples of their final drafts:

BOOK LINKS

How Much Is a Million? by David Schwartz (Mulberry Books, 1993)

The Story of Numbers and Counting, by Anita Ganeri (Oxford University Press, 1996)

Student Poems

NUMBERS
by Matt Nadel

Numbers on the ground
Numbers in the air
Numbers, numbers
    Everywhere

Flight numbers
Street signs
Shoe sizes, too
    I like numbers
How about you?

We use them on ovens
We use them on clocks
We use them when it's
    time to count our socks

We use them on license plates
We use them on walks
They give us the time
    when we look at clocks

Measuring nutrition
Clothing sizes, too
Numbers help us
    in everything we do!

NUMBERS IN MY HEAD
by Brett Menter

When you walk into lunch
    and you're saying "Hello!"
    you tell them your lunch number
    and you get Jell-O

When I start to sit down
    and my pants are too tight
    you tell your mom
    that the size is not right

I always remember
    that special date
    April 8th
    when I slid into home plate

When you start being lazy
    and your teacher gives you the look
    then you should open your math book
    to page 57 and take a look

Now you can see
    that numbers are all around
    in the air
    on the ground!

And I wake up

Poetry Page

MARVELOUS MATH
by Rebecca Kai Dotlich

How fast does a New York taxi go?
What size is Grandpa's attic?
How old is the oldest dinosaur?
The answer's in mathematics!

How many seconds in an hour?
How many in a day?
What size are the planets in the sky?
How far to the Milky Way?

How fast does lightning travel?
How slow do feathers fall?
How many miles to Istanbul?
Mathematics knows it all!

MATH ADVICE
by David L. Harrison

Be exact when you subtract
Lest you lose a digit,
Concentrate and sit up straight
And never twitch or fidget.
I knew a lad (and this is sad)
Who took eighteen from twenty,
Got a one when he was done
And figured that was plenty.
The moral here is pretty clear,
Never lose a digit!
Be precise and check it twice
Or you'll feel like an idgit.

TAKE A NUMBER
by Mary O'Neil

Imagine a world
Without mathematics:

No rulers or scales,
No inches or feet,
No dates or numbers
On house or street,
No prices or weights,
No determining heights,
No hours running through
Days and nights.
No zero, no birthdays
No way to subtract
All of the guesswork
Surrounding the fact.
No size for shoes,
Or suit or hat . . .
Wouldn't it be awful
To live like that?

Using the Power of Poetry to Teach Language Arts, Social Studies, Science, and More *Scholastic Professional Books*

Numbers Please!

As you're riding in your car, riding to school on the bus, or just walking around the house, take time to jot down all the ways that you see numbers being used.

In the spaces below, please list your discoveries. Have fun!

_____

_____

_____

_____

_____

_____

_____

_____

_____

_____

_____

_____

_____

_____

_____

_____

_____

You may also use the back of this sheet.

FROM KATHY'S CLASSROOM

Geometry

Focus Lesson:

Good writers sometimes collect data and place it into categories.
They use the data as a springboard for a poem

• • • • • •

Day One (30–45 minutes)

Setting the Stage

It is three weeks before school ends and I'm excited about teaching the final math unit of the year—geometry!

I begin the lesson by asking my students to get out their math logs as I write, "What is geometry?" on the overhead. I give them a few minutes to jot down their ideas and then it is time for the class to share.

"It is shapes," says Ryan.

"It is rectangles, squares, pentagons, circles, and rectangular prisms," adds Hayden while looking at the geometry poster that has been hanging in our classroom all year.

"Excellent thoughts and ideas!" I say. "Geometry may be flat objects like squares and rectangles, which is called 'plane geometry,' and it may also be three-dimensional objects, such as spheres, cubes, and pyramids.

"Today we are going on a 'discovery hunt.' We will begin right here in our classroom. I am going to pass out a Geometric Shapes reproducible (page 90). Please clip this sheet to your clipboard and write your name on it. You are now going to search for circles, squares, rectangles, and triangles. I want you to find as many items as you can for each category."

"Look everywhere—on the floor, walls, and ceiling," I encourage them. "Remember to observe with your eyes, not your mouths. If necessary, you may use the back of your reproducible to add items for one of the four categories, or you may develop a new category. Good luck!"

After spending a few minutes in our room, my class begins to explore other places in our school—the cafeteria, the entryway, the library. All class members busily write as many items as they can before it is time to return to the room.

Materials Suggested

- Math logs
- Clipboards and pencils
- Geometric Shapes reproducible (page 90)

I say, "You may put your sheets in your desk or you may take it home to add items that you discover there. Just remember to bring it back if you take it home tonight!"

Day Two *(30–45 minutes)*

Teaching the Focus Lesson and Writing the Poem

I begin the day by putting the focus lesson on the easel and saying aloud, "Good writers sometimes collect data and place it into categories. They use the data as a catalyst for a poem."

"If you think about it," I continue, "placing data into categories is what we did yesterday when we searched for objects of different shapes. Let's get out those sheets and share them in groups of three or four. If you hear a good idea, you may add it to your list." The students break into groups and share their ideas.

After ten minutes, I ask the class to come to the easel. I say, "You have done a wonderful job collecting and sharing your geometric information. Now I want you to take your data and use it as inspiration for a poem."

"On this assignment, you may work by yourself or you may work with a partner. You may choose one geometric category from your reproducible or you may choose more than one. You may write a list poem, a humorous poem, or a poem for two voices where both of you contribute your ideas to the poem. Good luck and have fun!"

Day Three *(60–90 minutes)*

Sharing and Writing the Final Product

Early the next morning, I have the individual poets and the partner poets read over their drafts and make the necessary changes. Next, I have them work in groups of four to listen to one another's poems, then revise and edit them. Lastly, they sign up with me for final polishing and publishing.

These poems are mounted on a geometric shape of their choice and displayed on a bulletin board entitled "We Live in a Geometric World."

BOOK LINKS

A Cloak for the Dreamer, by Aileen Friedman (Pearson, 1995)

Grandfather Tang's Story, by Ann Tompert (Crown, 1990)

The Greedy Triangle, by Marilyn Burns (Pearson 1995)

Pigs on the Ball, by Amy Axelrod (Aladdin Paperbacks, 1998)

Geometric Shapes

Directions: Look around and you'll see shapes everywhere. Write down items that are shaped like rectangles, circles, triangles, and squares in the boxes below.

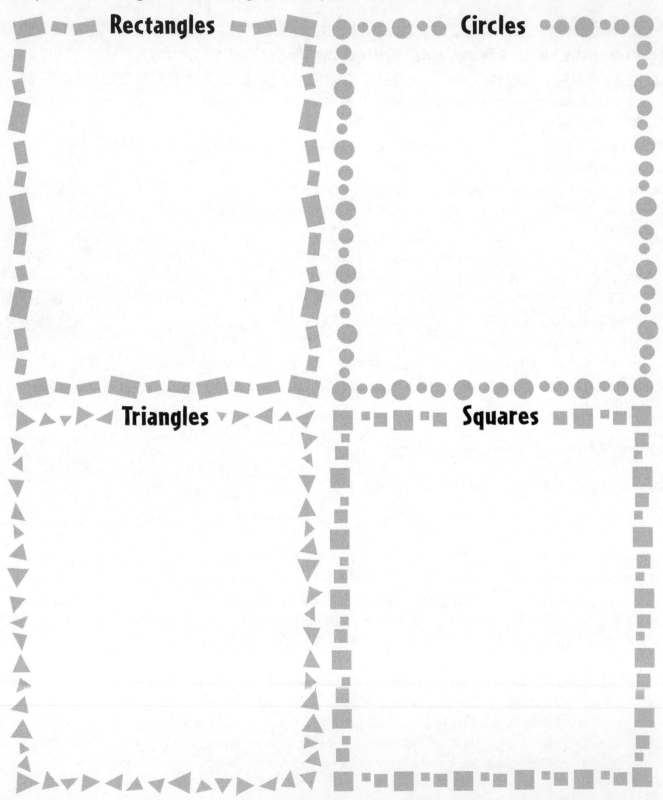

Rectangles

Circles

Triangles

Squares

Using the Power of Poetry to Teach Language Arts, Social Studies, Science, and More *Scholastic Professional Books*

CHAPTER 6

Sharing the Planet

Examining Interdependence in the Environment

We should take care of
the world we live in
because it would smell
like a pig if we didn't.

–Ben, Grade 1

We mean for this chapter to draw students into studying environments, including their own. The rain forest and the ocean are universally fascinating subjects. By the time you complete these units, you'll have a class full of experts who will care passionately about the animals they've chosen to research and the habitats in which those creatures live.

The mini unit leads them from far off places to much closer to home— directly into their own neighborhood. Armed with their developing skills of observation, research, and reflection, we think you'll see some inspired poetry based on students' heightened awareness of nature and how they fit into it.

FROM KATHY'S CLASSROOM

Rain Forest Rhapsody

Researching Animals of the Rain Forest

Materials Suggested

- A bulletin board depicting the layers of the rain forest with the various plants and animals that are found in each layer
- *Rain Forest Activity Book*, by Robin Bernard (Scholastic Inc., 1996) (optional)
- Rain forest cassette or CD
- Butcher paper for KWL *(know, want to find out, learned)* chart
- Three-prong pocketed folder for each child
- Various nonfiction books about the rain forest (preferably with illustrations)
- Assorted videos and movies about the rain forest
- *The New York Public Library Kid's Guide to Research*, by Deborah Heiligman (Scholastic Inc. 1998) (optional)
- Poems: "The Amazon" by David Harrison (page 102); "Sloths: A Poem for Two Voices" by David Harrison (page 103)
- One or two packs of five-by-eight-inch cards
- Rubric for Rain Forest Animal Poems (page 104)

With its tapestry of sights, sounds, and colors, this rain forest science unit immediately captivates students and draws them in. They are mesmerized by the hundreds of exotic plants, animals, birds, and insects found in every layer of these tropical places.

This unit provides an exciting backdrop for children to learn research and data-collecting skills using videos, books, the library, and the Internet. They take their information and weave it into poetry about some of nature's most intriguing animals. A helpful rubric assists them in measuring their own success.

Focus Lessons:

- Good writers learn how to collect information on note cards.
- Good writers sometimes incorporate factual information into their poetry.
- Good writers incorporate elements of good writing into their poetry.
- Good writers incorporate elements found in a rubric.

■ ■ ■ ■ ■ ■ ■

Poet's Note

Kathy's students are choosing creatures of the rain forest to be the subjects for poems. She wants them to learn about interdependence among species. I think it's a great way to make biology fun. I'm also reminded that association is a curious road without markers or maps. You never know where it will take you but you always wind up some-where. When Kathy says, "rain forest," I am immediately back aboard the riverboat La Amatista *in 1999, chugging up the Amazon River. On that trip I learned about a jungle soap opera starring a handsome but clueless weaverbird, egg-sucking monkeys, parasitic botflies, wasps in the protection racket, and freeloading cowbirds. Kathy's students may discover other intriguing relationships as they make notes and write their poems.*

Kathy invited me to contribute a rain forest poem. Watching a sloth near the top of a tall jungle cecropia tree was one of the thrills of my trip. Silhouetted against an amethyst-blue sky, the creature gazed down on us, distant and remote, as deliberately as a bored monarch on a leafy throne. I decided to write about that.

While writing, I concentrated on the elements of the memory—chattering parakeets diving in and out of the green canopy, a brown river, excited whispers, heat, isolation, sloth—and my thoughts turned serious.

My muse, however, felt impish. Without setting out to, I wrote a tongue-in-cheek poem for two (sloth) voices. Ah, well. I've learned not to argue. I sent the poem to Kathy and hoped her students would like it.

Such is the surprising versatility of poetry. Even when we care deeply about a subject, our poem may want to go at it lightly. I hope Kathy's students discover the same phenomenon. It is, I think, a delightful reminder. Poetry can be and should be used as a tool for learning about any subject. Yet it always remains true to its own nature. Poetry is a cat that purrs on its own terms. It never loses its capacity to surprise you, even when you're the poet.

BOOK LINKS

Rain Forest

40 Rubrics and Checklists to Assess Reading and Writing, by Adele Fiderer (Scholastic Inc., 1999)

Rain Forest, by Robin Bernard (Scholastic Inc., 1999)

Resourceful Rain Forest, by Pat and Barbara Ward (Mark Twain Media, 1998)

The New York Public Library Kid's Guide to Research, by Deborah Heiligman (Scholastic Inc., 1998)

A Unit About Tropical Rainforests, by Debby DePauw (Evan-Moore, 1994)

Before beginning this unit, I went to a local teacher supply store and purchased a large tropical rain forest bulletin board that showed the four layers of the forest and the various plants and animals found in each level.

Being the book junkie that I am, I visited several children's bookstores. Eureka! I found a wonderful resource book by Robin Bernard entitled *Rain Forest.* It is a treasure trove of information and activities that will help anyone to launch this unit successfully. I left the store armed with this sourcebook and several other rain forest books filled with glorious illustrations.

An excellent alternative is a quick trip to your local or school library. Our school librarian, Mrs. Schwinkendorf, has been an invaluable resource for me. She pulls books off our library shelves and, if necessary, does a district-wide search in order to find appropriate books and magazines. I place rain forest books and magazines everywhere in my class—in baskets, in tubs, on top of bookcases, and on shelves!

Mr. Heimbigner, our technology expert extraordinaire, helps the children do "safe" Internet searches during our library time. At the end of the unit, we collect the Internet research information and Mrs. Schwinkendorf stores it in a special "rain forest file" to be used again by future classes.

The following lessons focus on ways to help students gain background knowledge about the rain forest. You will learn strategies to help students gather research information and guide them through reading, writing, and presenting rain forest animal poetry. I also include a rubric for assessing poems that you might find beneficial.

Day One   (60 minutes or less)

Setting the Stage

When my class settles down, I say, "I'd like everyone to close your eyes and relax." As the children follow my directions, I play a rain forest CD with music that has exotic birds calling and animals making background sounds. The music fills our room.

"You are no longer in Room 12. You are now in a huge tropical rain forest located in South America. Think about what you see and how the weather feels. Which animals are near you and which animals are in the distance? Please keep your eyes closed. I want to share a beautiful poem that Mr. Harrison wrote." I proceed to read "The Amazon" (page 102). "Can you picture the scene? In a minute, I want you to open your eyes."

"Now slowly open your eyes. Look around our room. Do you notice anything new?"

"I see a bulletin board with rain forest plants and animals," mentions Chase.

"I notice that there are labels on some of the plants and animals," adds Allie.

"There are books everywhere!" says Rachel.

"Yes, you're right. You've all made excellent observations! Today we are going to begin studying about the interdependence of plants and animals in a tropical biome—the rain forest."

"I would like to find out what you know about the rain forest and what questions you have. In a few days, you are going to select an animal that you would like to research. And each of you is going to become an expert! I can't wait to see which animal you decide to study!"

"Can I choose mine today?" asks Chris.

"No, you have to wait," I reply.

I tape a large piece of butcher paper to the chalkboard on which I have written the following categories:

K	W	L
What we know about the tropical rain forest	**What we want to find out** about the tropical rain forest	**What we've learned about** the tropical rain forest

"Is there anyone who is willing to start?" I ask.

"I think that there are different kinds of rain forests," begins McKenna. I put her answer under the first category.

"I studied about the rain forest at my other school. I researched the sloth and he's real slow!" shares Khalil. I add Khalil's bit of information under the first category, too. As other children chime in, I carefully record what they say.

Next, it's on to what they want to find out. Again I script the questions carefully. They ask things like: What is the smallest monkey? How fast are jaguars in the jungle? How often does it rain in a rain forest?

I say that, during this unit, we are going to have many questions and we will discover many fascinating facts. "As you think of questions and as you find answers, please let me know. I will add your questions and answers to our categories." When the child finds the answer, he shows it to me, and I write his response and put his name in parenthesis under his answer. Throughout the unit, the butcher paper remains a permanent fixture in our classroom. It is a daily reminder of our quest for knowledge. The children learn that one of the most important lessons in the classroom is to ask many questions and strive to find the answers.

Week One *(60 minutes or less)*

Building a Strong Knowledge Base

The next several days are filled with a flurry of activity. I give students note taking sheets (page 73) to place in their three-prong pocketed folder. The children use these sheets to take notes as they read about and watch videos on the rain forest and its inhabitants. We spend about 30 to 40 minutes a day reading, writing, and asking questions about the rain forest. At times I put a copy of one of these informational pages on the overhead and model filling out the sheet. Their reading and note taking help them learn about the different layers of the rain forest and the plants and animals that live within them.

Then they add 10 to 15 sheets of lined paper. During the unit, the lined paper can be used for a variety of purposes, such as note taking during lectures or when watching a video. The rain forest model poems by both the children

BOOK LINKS

Rain Forest

The Great Kapok Tree, by Lynne Cherry (Gulliver, 1990)

Nature's Green Umbrella: Tropical Rain Forests, by Gail Gibbons (Morrow, 1994)

One Day in the Tropical Rain Forest, by Jean Craighead George (Harper Trophy, 1995)

Rain Forest, by Elinor Greenwood (Dorling Kindersly, 2001)

Rain Forest, by Barbara Taylor (Funfax Books, 1998)

Rain Forest Babies, by Kathy Darling (Walker and Company, 1997)

Rainforest Birds, by Bobbie Kalman (Crabtree Publishing Company, 1998)

Rainforest Wildlife, by Antonia Cunningham (EDC Publications, 1993)

Tropical Rainforests, by Jean Hamilton (Silver Burdett, 1995)

and adults go into the folder after the lined paper. Using crayons and/or marking pens, the students write their name and a title on the cover of the folder and then proceed to decorate it with brightly colored rain forest scenes.

Shortly into the second or third day of our study, I ask students to turn to the poetry section of their folders. We begin by sharing the poems aloud. Sometimes I begin reading and have my students echo-read. I may begin with a previously written student poem, such as "King of the Sky" by Courtney Harrison, or other selected poems that demonstrate the elements in our rubric.

I make certain that there are several selections and that they show different forms and styles. I then ask, "What do you notice? Spend a little time discussing the poems with the students in your group. You may want to choose one person to be your recorder and jot down a few observations that your group discovers."

After a few minutes, I ring a bell and call the class to attention. I ask, "What did you learn from your discussion?" On the chalkboard I list their discoveries:

1. All of the poems are about rain forest animals.

2. Mr. Harrison's poem is for two people (or two sloths) to read.

3. There is colorful language (good word choice).

4. Many of them have strong verbs.

The list goes on and on. I say, "After you have finished your research, I want you to write magnificent poems about your special animal." This announcement gives students added incentive to discover interesting facts about rain forest animals.

Every Afternoon | (40–45 minutes)

(25 minutes: book share and discussion; 20 minutes: silent reading time)

Each day after lunch I set aside time to read to my class. I begin by saying, "As I read one rain forest book to you and share other rain forest books that you might choose to read during quiet reading time today, think about the animal that you are most interested in researching. Please have a second choice in mind because I want everyone to have a *different* animal."

I then proceed to read, and we discuss one book. During the next several afternoons, I repeat the same process. My class especially loves *The Great Kapok Tree* by Lynne Cherry, *Rain Forest Babies* by Kathy Darling, and *Nature's Green Umbrella: Tropical Rain Forests* by Gail Gibbons. (See page 95 for additional resources.)

After our discussion, I introduce several new rain forest library books and magazines and give a short book talk about each one. I mention once more that it is important to think about selecting an animal that is well known. Nothing is more frustrating for a child than not being able to find enough information! Some of the animals my students have researched include sloths, orangutans, jaguars, toucans, gorillas, howler monkeys, tree frogs, and macaws.

Every afternoon, during the silent reading time that follows our discussions, my class devours the literature, searching for their "special" animal.

Week Two (60 minutes)

Selection of Animals; Focus Lesson on How to Introduce Categories for Note Taking on Research Cards

After a week or so of being immersed in rain forest life, I want my students to choose a specific animal on which to focus in depth. I place five-by-eight-inch index cards and a paper clip on each child's desk. "Today," I announce, "each of you is going to select a special animal and become a rain forest researcher. You will learn how to label five-by-eight-inch index cards and how to collect and record data or information."

I get out a clipboard and attach our class list to it. I call each child's name one by one, and each one tells me which animal he or she would like to study. Chris chooses a sugar glider, while Shelby selects the delicate marmoset. The children have been given the gift of time, and they have made wise choices.

"Now we are ready for our next step. Please get out a pencil. Who can tell me something that you might want to find out about your animal?" Using the overhead, I begin to list the information:

1. Physical characteristics

2. Habitat (where my animal lives)

3. Who are its enemies?

4. Special features or special behaviors

5. Interesting facts or unique characteristics

6. Food

7. References (here I found my information)

I say, "On each card, list one category and number it. Then turn your cards over and write your name on the back of every card. During the next week, you will be gathering information. I would like you to have at least three different references. You will take this information and develop it into a beautiful and informative poem. Later on, each of you will make a giant rain forest animal paper pillow. They will be hung all over our room." The excitement builds.

Modeling How to Collect and Record Information Using Bullets

It is time to move to our easel. There I take out a rain forest animal book, find an animal that hasn't been selected by anyone in our class, and begin reading about it. After I finish reading, I write *Physical Characteristics* on the easel. Under it, I have the class contribute ideas gleaned about the animal. I use a bullet for each point. I say, "What do you notice about each bullet or point?"

"I notice that you only use a few words," observes Melissa.

"That's right. I am just jotting down ideas. Some of the information will be useful later when you're developing your rain forest poems. I want you to find at least six facts for this category. Some of the other categories will have a smaller number."

Then I go to the next category, *Habitat*, and we continue the process. By having the students use bullets when they are researching, you are going to hear the child's voice when the poem is written, not the encyclopedia speaking.

After we finish working on the habitat category, I conclude, "I hope that all of you understand what should be written on your research cards. If you have any questions, please ask me."

An example for the physical characteristics of a gorilla might look like this:

Physical Characteristics

* Largest of apes

* Superb eyesight

* Group leader has silvery hair on his back (he's called a silverback)

* Males weigh 450 pounds

* Males are nearly six feet tall

For the next several days, the class is immersed in the process. They have their parents take them to public libraries; they explore our school library; they browse through magazines; they call the Denver Zoo; they surf the Internet.

During this time, it is my job to help with the hunt, to be the cheerleader, to give guidance and encouragement to the more fragile learners. It is an amazing process. When you give children a choice, they become empowered. They fall in love with their animal! They want to learn, and they can't wait to come to school!

Another Day in Week Two (45 minutes)

The Rubric Focus Lesson

I find that introducing a rubric for this poetry writing lesson provides structure and direction for my students. The rubric (page 104) spells out for students what elements I expect them to include in their poems. It allows me to focus on those elements and not grade the way they say something.

The important thing is to introduce the rubric for their animal poems before they begin writing their poems. I give a copy of the rubric to everyone and put a copy of it on the overhead. We discuss the elements of the rubric as a class. This is a perfect time to share two or three of the previously written student poems.

I say, "Look at the rubric and then look carefully at Katie's poem." I ask, "Which elements does Katie include in her poem?"

Ben responds, "She has a very creative title. You want to find out which animal is the Silk of the Amazon."

Matt adds, "She includes so many physical characteristics, such as its long tail, its brown fur, and its big sharp teeth."

As Ben and Matt make comments, I write their observations on the overhead. I tell students to keep the rubric in their folder and refer to it often. They now have the tools, and they are ready to start.

Another Day in Week Two (25–30 minutes)

Drafting

"Today you are going to write the rough draft of your poem," I begin. "First, I want you to skim and scan your research cards. Then look over the rubric and look over the model poems. Spend some time thinking about your chosen animal and what you want to say. Today you are just going to get your thoughts down on paper. Don't worry if you can't think of the title. Just write! During this time I want everyone to work silently. Good luck! Do your best job! Begin!"

After 15 to 20 minutes, I ask them to stop writing. The class shares in small groups for five or ten minutes. Class members may give suggestions.

The Next Day (30–45 minutes)

Focus Lesson on Elements of Good Writing: Revising

I being by saying, "Please come over to our easel. Today I want you to fine tune your draft. What are some of the elements of good writing?" I ask. As they contribute, I list them so that everyone can refer to them. Here are some of the suggestions:

- Have a unique title that tells about some aspect of the animal
- Use fresh language
- Incorporate an element of surprise
- Think of a good beginning and a good ending
- Choose strong verbs, not wimpy ones
- Vary the beginnings of your lines
- Use descriptive language, but select your words carefully
- Include a message about your animal

"Excellent ideas!" I say. "Now please take your poems from yesterday and reread them with these new ideas in mind. Remember, you might want to cross out, change, or add on. Refer to the suggestions that your classmates made and look at your rubrics. Do your best work!"

The Next Day (45 minutes)

Final Drafts

The class is now ready to type or write their final copies, and since they will be shared and displayed, they want to do an excellent job. They can see how their hard work has paid off. Here are a few student efforts:

Student Poems

THE BEST GLIDER
by Chris Treagesser
The sugar glider everybody
    knows
He comes
    And he goes
He glides and glides
    in the midnight skies
He eats fruit, nectar, sap,
    flowers
He's not so fast
He's not so slow
    but when you see him
He'll go, go, go
He lives in the trees
    with the greatest
    of ease
He lives in Australia
Because that's his home
This is the sugar glider
everyone should know

KING OF THE SKY
by Courtney Harrison
The harpy eagle zooms,
    Flips and twirls
You cannot see him
He's just a strip
    Of black and white
He flies at full speed
    With talons sparkling
Trying to catch parrots, macaws,
    Monkeys, sloths, and snakes
Living in tall trees
    Watching everything in sight
There's so much that
    The King of the Sky can do
I just can't show them
    All to you

Display Ideas

1. **Rain Forest Kaleidoscope.** Hang netting in your classroom or on the hall ceiling. In the netting hang a kaleidoscope of rain forest animals and plants, labeling as many items as possible. Have the animals hold the poems that were written about them.

2. **Animal Paper Pillows.** My teaching partner, Ann Connell-Allen, shared this idea with me. This project needs to have the supervision of a parent volunteer or the teacher.

    Select pictures of rain forest animals that your class has researched and make an overhead transparency of each animal. Cut off two large pieces of butcher paper per animal. Tape one piece of butcher paper onto a wall or the chalkboard. Save the other piece for later use.

    Put the animal transparency on an overhead and shine the overhead of the animal onto the butcher paper that has been taped to the wall. Using a pencil, the child then traces around the animal and marks in some of the animal's features. After the child completes this step, she places the butcher paper on the floor and, using a Sharpie, she begins to trace the outline and some of the inside details. She then uses crayons and/or oil pastels to color in the body of the animal.

    Next, the child puts her two pieces of butcher paper together and carefully cuts around the outline of the animal. Then, an adult will begin stapling and stuffing the animal with newspaper and/or scraps of the leftover butcher paper. Lastly, a label with the child's name and the name of the animal is stapled onto the completed animal. We hang the animals from the ceiling light fixtures using string and a large bent paper clip.

EXTENSION IDEAS

1. This unit can easily be adapted to another biome, such as the desert, the mountains, or the ocean. Children would compose poems about animals living in one of those regions.

2. Using their rain forest animal, have the students compose a poem for two voices using David Harrison's "Sloths" (page 103) as a model.

Poetry Page

THE AMAZON
by David L. Harrison

To paint you, I'd start with the sky
blue as a butterfly wing
then daub on yellow-brown clouds
speckled like bunches of aging bananas,
some furrowed fields of parched clay clouds
cracking open in the sun,
and maybe a thunderhead
with lightning in its eyes,
threatening a temper tantrum.

I'd paint the bank a deep reddish brown
like monkey fur or hawk feather,
a thin mud ribbon
where iguanas doze out sunny days
and caimans steal
when dark night comes.

For the jungle I'd paint
a squiggly green line around the water
like a baldheaded man
with a bushy fringe of curly hair
polka-dotted with bright birds
and dragonflies.

Only then would I paint you.
I'd hold my brush
with all the colors still in it
and paint you with that
so you'd be brown but textured
like a thick rich soup
strong enough to carry them all—
the sky of many moods and colors,
the green-haired jungle,
the hawk feather line—
to carry them all on your shoulders.
I wish I could paint all of that.

Using the Power of Poetry to Teach Language Arts, Social Studies, Science, and More *Scholastic Professional Books*

Poetry Page

SLOTHS
A Poem for Two Voices
by David L. Harrison

oh we know

slow we

and think

slow and

below

it takes

you're so

we only move

chew a leaf

few will do until

then we nap

toes

or two

knows

asleep

we finish

snore

we're sort of

blink

and go

never look

no

too long when

slow

enough to

or two a

we're through

and curl our

do we have three

who

we always fall

before

counting

snore

Rubric for Rain Forest Animal Poems

Name _____

Key Elements	Evaluative Criteria	Score
1. Physical characteristics	The poet includes at least three of the animal's physical characteristics.	
2. Habitat	The poet includes information about where the animal lives. It might include the level in the rain forest and the country or the continent.	
3. Food	The poet includes what type(s) of food the animal eats. This might include how often it eats.	
4. Interesting facts	The poet includes something in the poem that makes the animal unique or different from other animals.	
5. Title	The poet writes an interesting or intriguing title. It might be mysterious, one that makes the reader want to read on.	
6. Strong Verbs	The poet shows how the animal moves using carefully selected verbs.	

Total score _____

Comments: _____

_____

_____

_____

_____

Scoring Guide
3 = to a high degree
2 = to a satisfactory degree
1 = to a limited degree
0 = did not include this element

Using the Power of Poetry to Teach Language Arts, Social Studies, Science, and More *Scholastic Professional Books*

FROM KATHY'S CLASSROOM

Ocean Animals

Focus Lessons:

- Good writers write a factual poem using a first person perspective (I am . . .).
- Good writers reread their drafts carefully.
- Using a rubric, good writers incorporate key elements of writing into their poetry.

• • • • • • •

Day One (60 minutes or less)

Share

I begin this unit by placing a large piece of light-blue butcher paper on the front board. Using a blue marker, I draw a circle in the center and in it write "The Ocean."

"Please get out a piece of paper and jot down everything that has to do with the ocean. You have five minutes!" I say as I join in and write, too!

After five minutes, I say, "Stop!" then pass out a web graphic organizer to each child.

"Now I am going to put information on our class web while you put the ideas on your own web. Who has something that they'd like to share?" I ask.

Emily says, "Fish live in the ocean." I write the word "Fish" on the butcher paper, draw a circle around it and draw a line to connect it to the center "Ocean" circle. I ask the children to write "Fish" on their webs, draw a circle around it, and connect the fish circle to the center circle by drawing a straight line.

"Be more specific. What are some of the types of fish that live in the ocean?" I ask.

"Sharks!" says Matt.

"Barracudas," adds Genna.

I write each addition by adding spokes around the "fish" circle.

"Whales," mentions Katie.

"Are whales fish?" I ask.

"No," says Ben. "They are mammals." I start a new category entitled

Materials Suggested

- A bulletin board with a cutaway illustration that shows an underwater ocean scene, including various aquatic plants and animals that inhabit different levels of the ocean
- "Deep Sea Rap," by M.C. Goldish (Scholastic Inc., 1992) (page 110)
- The Magic School Bus On the Ocean Floor (Scholastic Inc., 1994)
- Various ocean CDs and cassettes (optional)
- Three-prong, pocketed folder for each child (I call this their "Captain's Log")
- Assorted videos about ocean plants and animals
- A wide variety of nonfiction books pertaining to the ocean and its animals (preferably with illustrations)
- Assorted student poems
- One or two packs of five-by-eight-inch cards
- Ocean Animal Rubric (page 111)

"Mammals" and draw a circle around it.

We continue the process for the next 10 to 15 minutes. I then close this lesson by saying, "Keep your webs in a safe place in your desks. As we acquire new information, we will add new categories to our webs."

The class web stays on the front board as a visual reminder throughout the unit. Periodically we revisit it, adding the students' latest discoveries.

Week One *(approximately 60 minutes per day, for 4 to 5 days)*

Building a Strong Knowledge Base

As with the rain forest unit, I spend about an hour a day during our first week building students' background knowledge. Students collect information in a three-prong folder we designate as "My Captain's Log." For the Read Alouds, I like to begin with *The Magic School Bus On the Ocean Floor*. This is a great book for teaching about nonfiction text features such as illustrations, diagrams, and labels. Students also read on their own and watch videos; some of my favorite resources are listed on the left. By the end of the week, students are brimming with information!

Week Two *(60 minutes or less)*

Selection of Ocean Animals and Note Taking on Research Cards

After we have worked on the ocean unit for a week or so, I have the class members select their special animals. I try to have each child pick a different sea mammal, fish, or bird. As with the rain forest unit, the children will then gather their information from a variety of sources. They use the classroom library, the public library, and do searches on the Internet. They check out science magazines.

I share with them the importance of collecting information from a variety of places. They keep their five-by-eight-inch research cards and their reference materials on their desks. They are intent on finding out everything they can about their animal of choice! They make every second count. It is my job to be a fact finder and an assistant, and to give help and encouragement to all those students who need a little extra support.

Another Day *(45 minutes)*

The Rubric Focus Lesson

After the children have been doing their research for several days, I say, "Soon, each of you is going to write a poem from a first person perspective. Today I would like you to look over the rubric that you will use while you're writing your poem" (page 111).

BOOK LINKS

Ocean Life

Deep Blue Sea Theme Digest (Scholastic Inc., 1992)

Endangered Ocean Animals, by Dave Taylor (Crabtree Publishing Co., 1992)

The Magic School Bus On the Ocean Floor, by Joanna Cole (Scholastic, 1994)

The New York Public Library Kid's Guide to Research, by Deborah Heiligman (Scholastic Inc., 1998)

NatureScope: Diving Into Oceans (McGraw-Hill, 1997)

Ocean Animals, by Michael Chinery (Random House, 1992)

Ocean Explorer, by Sue Nicholson (Tangerine Press, 2001)

Polar Animals, by Norman Barrett (Franklin Watts, Ltd., 1990)

Seals and Sea Lions, by Vicki Leon (Blake Publishing, Inc., 1988)

Tiger Sharks and Other Dangerous Animals, by Anita Ganeri (Kingfisher, 1995)

What is a Marine Animal? by Bobbie Kalman (Crabtree Publishing Co., 2000)

I put the rubric on the overhead and pass out an individual copy to everyone. I give them a short amount of time to look over the rubric and then say, "Look in the poetry section of your Captain's Log. Today we are going to read some student-written poems. Please turn to the first poem, 'Star of Antarctica' by Ryan Camp." We carefully read it aloud as a class.

I then say, "Please put your rubric next to the poem, and with one or two friends, read Ryan's poem aloud and then discuss which elements Ryan included. In a few minutes, we'll share the ideas as a class." As the teams get to work, I quietly circulate around the room.

After a few minutes, I put Ryan's poem on the overhead and I ask, "What are some of the elements from the rubric that Ryan included in his poem?"

"He included an interesting title," says Austin. "It made me want to find out why he thinks his penguin is a star." As Austin speaks, I write, "interesting title" on Ryan's poem on the overhead. I invite the children to write that information on their copies, if they'd like.

"Who else has something to add?" I ask.

"I noticed that he used strong verbs like *waddle* and *trudge* to describe the way his penguin moves," says Hailey.

"Great observation, Hailey."

Next, we read the second student-written poem aloud. Again, I place a copy on the overhead. I always try to have more than one sample so that they can compare and contrast. I want them to realize that words can be incorporated into poems in countless ways.

I end the lesson by telling the students to keep the rubric in their Captain's Log and to refer to it as they write their poems.

Now they are ready to compose!

Another Day (*(30–45 minutes)*

Focus Lesson and Drafting

"Good morning, wonderful class! Today you are going to begin writing the rough draft of your poem, but first I would like to share a focus lesson with you." As I talk, I write, "Good writers write a factual poem using a first person perspective. They <u>become</u> their animal. ('I am . . .')." I ask students to copy the focus lesson in their Captain's Log.

After they copy the focus lesson, I again put Ryan's poem on the overhead, and we share it aloud. "What do you notice about his poem?" I ask.

"He becomes the Adélie penguin. I feel like I'm with him in Antarctica," says Erik.

Student Poems

STAR OF THE ANTARCTIC
by Ryan Camp

I am the Adélie penguin
I swim with the wind
It carries me
    to the silvery ice
    of Antarctica!
As I waddle up
    onto the frozen floor
I must beware of my enemy
    the seal!
My black and white
    tuxedo dries
      quickly as I trudge up
        a mountain!
When I get to the top
    I toboggan back
      down!
As I'm coming down
    I shoot off from
      a diamond cliff
I dive into
    the frigid water
Swishing and swerving
    to catch my prey
      the squid and the krill!
At night
    I keep my eggs warm
My nest is made of rocks
    and almost anything
      I can get!
I pile them up
    like a miniature tower!
Then my eggs don't
    go rolling out
      and it keeps
    my babies warm
When the sun peeks out
    I jump off
      my nest
And let my mate
    take over
I am the Adélie penguin!

"You're right, Erik."

"Please get out your research cards. Look them over carefully. Then, as you're writing your rough draft today, I want you to become your animal. Share where you live and think about how you move. Think about what makes you unique or special. Just get your thoughts down. Do your best job!"

After 15 to 20 minutes, I ask the class to stop writing and share in small groups. I ask students to tell each poet one or two things that they think are positive about his or her poem. Then, on a sticky note, I ask them to jot down one suggestion that might improve the poem and hand it to the poet.

Another Day (30–45 minutes)

Rereading, Revising, and Using a Rubric

"Please come over to the easel," I begin. "Today you will actually have two focus lessons that go together very nicely." I proceed to write the following:

1. Good writers reread their drafts carefully and make revisions.

2. Using a rubric, good writers incorporate key elements of writing into their poetry.

We share the focus lessons aloud and then I review the idea that when writers revise they cross things out, they add on, and they look for careful word choice. I ask them to get out their rubric and use it to check off the elements as they finish their revisions. The last thing that the class does for this lesson is to buddy-share. Again I am a silent observer, and I am amazed when I hear their poetry.

Student Poem

FRAGILE FAIRY
by Rachel Sabey

I am the graceful
    Fairy Penguin
I swim every day
    at the bay
      If I get a chance
        to play
Australia and New Zealand
    are my homes
    from which
      I don't care
        to roam

I will fish for my dish
    of dinner today

I'm only eleven inches tall
    I seem so small

I am blue and gray
    the shades of the bay.

My enemies are
    lizards and snakes
    eagles and gulls
    rats and cats

On the land
    and in the sea
Please don't kill me

I love my sandy burrow
    because I can lay down
    and curl

Fragile fairy, fragile fairy
    the smallest of all
      the penguins in
        the world.

Display Ideas

1. **Ocean Mural** Using light blue butcher paper as background, make an underwater mural that can be displayed on a bulletin board in the classroom or on a wall in the hallway. The teacher and students paint waves at the top and sand and plant life at the bottom of the mural. Each child paints his or her ocean animal on a piece of construction paper, cuts it out, attaches the poem to the bottom of the animal, and tapes the animal and poem onto the mural. The display might be entitled "Under the Sea" or "The Ocean Is My Home!"

2. **Batik Ocean Animal Pillows** Working with the art teacher, have each child design his or her own ocean animal pillow. These pillows can be hung from the light fixtures by using a piece of ribbon or string.

3. **Plastic Wrap Underwater Scene** Have the child draw his or her animal, some rocks, and seaweed on a piece of construction paper using marking pens or watercolors. Next, the child cuts out the pieces. The teacher passes out two large pieces of plastic wrap to each child. The child puts the first piece of plastic wrap down on his desk and carefully places the sea animal and the accessories on top. After that, the child places the other piece of plastic wrap on top in order to seal the scene. Then, the child places a narrow folded strip of blue construction paper on the top of the scene and another narrow strip at the bottom of the scene. The strips are stapled in place to form a frame. Lastly, the child attaches a piece of yarn to the top of the scene. Now the pictures are ready to be hung from the light fixtures.

Extension Ideas

1. Take a field trip to the ocean, if possible.

2. Take a field trip to an aquarium, preferably one that has an educational program with hands-on experiences and guided tours. The field trip can either be an introduction to the unit or a culminating activity.

3. Invite a guest speaker to share information about possible careers pertaining to the ocean (working as an oceanographer, a marine botanist, a marine biologist, an artist, and so on).

4. Have your class perform science experiments that deal with salt water.

5. Have your students research and discuss problems, such as oil spills, overbuilding along the shores, overfishing, pollution, and boating accidents, and possible solutions to these problems.

6. Brainstorm with your class on treasures that we receive from the sea, such as salt, shells, sponges, hydropower, fish, and pearls. Ask how humans use these treasures.

7. Have students make up riddles about sea animals. The students write three clues on a piece of paper. They then write the answer on the paper and cover the answer by taping a flap over it, and proceed to quiz their classmates.

> The gift of the sea is a gift to all life . . . . If you undermine the health of the oceans, you undermine the health of our future.
>
> –Sylvia Earle

Poetry Page

DEEP SEA RAP

by M.C. Goldish

It's a beautiful day, well, don't you agree?
Perfect for a dive into the deep blue sea!
Put on your gear, get set to explore,
Travel from the surface to the ocean floor.
Start at the top, where the seaweed has grown,
You're in the upper layers of the intertidal zone.
Follow that snail all wrapped in curls,
Look! There's an oyster with a string of pearls!
Talk with the clam, and sit with the worm,
The clam'll clam up, but the worm will squirm.
Salute the starfish, smile at the crab,
And feel those mussels—not an ounce of flab!

CHORUS:
Dive on down! Seaward bound!
Commotion in the ocean is all around!
Dive on down! Seaward bound!
Commotion in the ocean is all around!

Go a little deeper, where the sunlight loses tone,
You're entering the waters of the shallow-ocean zone.
Don't scare the puffer, or before your very eyes
It'll puff itself up to twice its normal size!
Wink at the octopus with ink so dark,
Dance with the flounder, but don't pet the shark!
What's that wiggling?
 A shock you feel?
Welcome to the stun of the electric eel.
Cuddle with the cuttlefish, shake with the squid.
(Or don't do either, but say that you did!)
Watch how the man-of-war floats on by,
While the anchovy's dreaming of a pizza pie!

CHORUS:
Dive on down! Seaward bound!
Commotion in the ocean is all around!
Dive on down! Seaward bound!
Commotion in the ocean is all around!

Sink to the bottom of the dark unknown,
Walk along the floor of the open-ocean zone.
See that lantern fish—wow, what a glow!
It helps with no sunlight down below!
Are those baby shrimp? Guess again—they're krill.
Fish like to eat 'em, and a lot of them will!
Wave to the viperfish, down so far,
But beware of the dragonfish and brittle star.
Who takes the size prize? The blue whale does,
Larger than a dinosaur ever was!
Say good-bye to the hagfish, and squeeze the sponge,
You've reached the very bottom of your deep-sea plunge!

CHORUS:
Dive on down! Seaward bound!
Commotion in the ocean is all around!
Dive on down! Seaward bound!
Commotion in the ocean is all around!

Using the Power of Poetry to Teach Language Arts, Social Studies, Science, and More   *Scholastic Professional Books*

Name _____ Date _____

Ocean Animal Rubric

Name _____ Date _____

Name _____ Date _____

Score

	Score
I. Physical Characteristics The poem includes at least two of the animal's physical characteristics.	
2. Habitat The poem includes information on where the animal lives.	
3. Food The poem includes what type(s) of food the animal eats. It also might include how often it eats.	
4. Interesting facts The poem includes something that shows how the animal is unique or different from other animals.	
5. Title The poem includes an interesting or intriguing title. The title may be mysterious. It makes the reader want to read on.	
6. Strong verbs The poem uses carefully selected verbs to show how the animal moves.	
7. Lines The poem includes a variety of beginning words and/or phrases that make the poem interesting.	
8. First person The poem is written from a first person ("I") perspective.	

Comments: _____

_____

_____

_____

Scoring Guide
4 = to a high degree
3 = to a satisfactory degree
2 = to a limited degree
I = did not include this element

FROM KATHY'S CLASSROOM

Environmental Encounters

Using Our Senses to Explore Nature

We should take care of the world we live in. It was beautiful and wild for our ancestors, it is beautiful and wild for us now, and it should be beautiful and wild for our descendants.

–Jennifer, Grade 8

Poet's Note

I've been in some beautiful libraries, many of them clean, well ordered, and filled with great books and displays. But one of the most interesting places I've seen was an old-fashioned library in a run-down building greatly in need of bricks-and-mortar attention. The librarian was a collector. My initial impression was that I was in the junk room of the world's foremost pack rat. Countertops were lined with cages, bowls, and containers that were home to mice, gerbils, hamsters, birds, and fish. The place was brimming with birds' nests and butterflies, feathers and skins shed by snakes, shiny-looking rocks and colorful leaves. And children!

Mrs. B.'s reputation as a nature lover was known far and wide. Her library was the place to be. Students could hardly wait to get there each day to see what Mrs. B. had brought for them to see. Everyone had an assignment: check on the fish, refill water dishes, feed the toad. Some brought their own contributions to add to the odds and ends of nature.

Kathy reminds me of that insightful librarian who gave her children so much to look at and touch and think about. But Kathy takes the next important step. She encourages her children to write about their sensations. Right on! Or, in this case, write on!

Materials Suggested

- Collection of items from nature
- Easel
- Writers' notebooks
- Poems: "High Country" and "Crossing Paths," by David L. Harrison; "Live Oak" by Kathy Holderith (page 115)

This mini unit follows the units on the rain forest and ocean naturally in that it stimulates students to practice what they've been learning, and it provides them with a chance to actually observe the subjects they will write about.

Teacher and poet Shelley Harwayne says that we need to show children the roots of writing, not just the blossoms. At the beginning of the year, I set up a center that has a wide variety of items (at least 30) from nature. (I have lichen, seashells, interesting rocks, leaves, and more.) I have a basket filled with magnifying glasses in the center, too. I also invite the class to bring in things they have collected to add to our center.

Many of my students spend a great deal of spare time in our Colorado mountains. I encourage them to take their writers' notebooks with them and record the beautiful or mysterious things that they see. Wherever you live and teach—in a rural, suburban, or urban setting—children love to discover ways to encounter nature.

Focus Lesson:

Good writers think about their relationship with nature
and learn to write about their feelings.

■ ■ ■ ■ ■ ■ ■

Day One *(20 minutes)*

Setting the Stage

I move to the collection of nature items and select one item. I ask the class to come over to the easel.

"What can you observe about this item?" I ask my students. "Look carefully and tell me what you see. We'll make a list of what you observe."

I examine the item thoughtfully and jot down a few of my own observations in front of the class. I invite the children to help make contributions and I add their ideas to my list.

We discuss the five senses. I mention that they shouldn't use the sense of taste because of sanitary issues.

I share a nature poem or two, such as David's "High Country" (page 115). We talk about how sometimes poets see things in a different light or they observe things that others simply pass by. I tell my students that teacher-poet Shelley Harwayne says, "Writers lead nosy lives."

I tell my class that tomorrow each student will select an item from the center, or choose something they have seen on a walk, and begin to write a poem about it in their writers' notebooks.

Day Two *(30 minutes)*

Drafting the Poems

The next day I give my students a few minutes to select an object to write about from the nature center collection. I remind them that they are also free to choose to write about some other encounter they have had in nature.

I read another nature poem, such as David's "Crossing Paths" (page 115), and remind everyone of what we talked about the previous day, that poets observe things carefully in order to write about what they see and how they feel.

I set the timer for ten minutes and the class writes. At the end of the ten minutes, they share ideas in small groups or with the entire class.

I go around the room, congratulating and encouraging. I want the students to become excited about their initial efforts. I remind them that these poems are only their first drafts. I say that writers take their first efforts and revise to make them even better.

At the end of this period, I say that tomorrow we will write our final drafts in class and then take turns reading them. I promise to read one that I have written, too.

Day Three   *(20–30 minutes)*

Sharing and Revising the Poems

I ask the class to put away everything on their desks and get comfortable. We are about to celebrate our encounters with nature by reading the poems we've written. I volunteer to start our presentation by reading my poem about an oak tree I observed on a recent walk.

When I finish reading, I ask for one or two positive comments about my poem. Is there something in my poem that makes the listener think? Does it make students want to know more? I use this to model how we will respond to the other poems that we are about to enjoy.

The students then take turns reading their own poems. When we finish (sometimes it takes longer than one period to hear all of the poems and offer comments), we discuss what we should do with so many fine poems. We might decide to decorate our board in the hall with them and add pictures and drawings about nature. To do that, each student will need a fresh sheet of paper to copy his or her poem from the writer's notebook. I like this process because penmanship tends to improve on the display copy, and a few more revisions creep into the final version.

Poetry Page

HIGH COUNTRY
by David L. Harrison

High country sings its own wind-song
of flowers dressed for spring's brief fling,
snow-water breaking on ledges.

Wind-song sings
of eagles winging canyon walls,
salmon leaping falls,
caribou bands spread under stars,
solitary moose in marshes.

High country sings its own wind-song
of nights that chill and days that burn.
"Leave if you must," it sings, "but you'll return."

CROSSING PATHS
by David L. Harrison

A single hoof-mark
in the moist trail

Small
probably a deer

We'll never meet
yet our paths cross
here

In these woods
our separate ways
are clear

But standing briefly
where this deer stood

Is a memory
worth taking
beyond the woods

LIVE OAK
by Kathy Holderith

Did you spring
from a seed
in an open field
with no houses
around to
obstruct your view?

How old are you
and what impact
have the years
had on you?

When did lichen
begin to cling to
you?

How many birds
have made nests
in your leaves?

Which animals
have found shelter
on the ground at
your feet?

Do you enjoy
the summer sun
or does it drain you?

Do the winter winds
that howl
chill you to your bone?

And one final
question, Live Oak,
Are you afraid
to die?

CHAPTER 7

We're Here! We're Here!

Expressing Ourselves Through Poetry

What I've learned so far is how to paint a rainbow.
–Janette, Grade 1

T his, we think, is a fun chapter filled with experiences to help children identify with the world we live in. From thinking and writing about sunny thoughts, to learning how to let their imagination roam from one connection to another, to trying to be funny by developing their own style, the lessons provided are light and entertaining.

FROM KATHY'S CLASSROOM

Sunny Poetry

Using a Web to Explore Thoughts

In this unit, students work with the idea of webbing as a useful tool in collecting their thoughts and seeing relationships. Writing sunny poems gives children a chance to think about what makes them happy and helps them put their feelings into words.

Sunny poetry also provides a simple method (complete with form) that you can use to assist students in their efforts to critique their writing and look for ways to improve.

Focus Lesson:

Good writers sometimes web ideas to help collect and organize their thoughts.

■ ■ ■ ■ ■ ■ ■

Sunny thoughts. . . Just say it, and for an adult it conjures up memories of strolling along the ocean shore on a bright August day, hiking on a shaded mountain trail in Montana, having a leisurely dinner with close friends. But mention sunny thoughts to children and the definition changes dramatically. For children "sunny thoughts" might be kicking the winning goal in a soccer game, riding a bike down a steep hill, performing in a dance recital, or playing with a Labrador puppy on a Saturday afternoon.

Day One   (60 minutes or less)

Setting the Stage and Sharing Poems

To begin this lesson I say, "Today I want you to think about a sunny time that you've had in your life. It might be a trip to the mountains, a day at the pool, or an exciting game of hockey."

I share, "I have so many sunny memories in my life. Among my sunny memories are the times my sister, Liz, and I enjoyed days at Redondo Beach with our cousin, Jerry. We spent many hot summer days playing volleyball, strolling along the coast, savoring taquitos and chocolate shakes, and riding powerful waves into shore. After bodysurfing, we flopped on our towels and let the sun warm us."

Materials Suggested

@ Writers' notebooks

@ Poems: "Sunflakes" by Frank Asch, "Sun Games" by David Harrison (see page 121)

@ One large piece of yellow butcher paper

@ Two Strengths and One Change Form (sample on page 119)

"Books have always been an important part of my life as well. Another sunny memory I have is of riding my bike to our small library, checking out as many books as possible, racing home, and immediately beginning to read my latest piece of literature while devouring mint chocolate chip ice cream."

I add, "Now I want you to close your eyes and think about a sunny memory that you have."

After a minute or two, I ask, "Does anyone have a sunny thought that you would be willing to share?" Everyone's hand goes up! Everyone has a story to tell!

After we share some sunny thoughts, I ask the class to get out their Poetry-Song folders and I pass out the poems by Ach and Harrison (page 121), as well as the student-written poems. They place the poems in their folders, and then we read the poems aloud.

It's amazing what a powerful model the student poems are. The children think, If Khalil can write this well, so can I.

To keep my class on their toes, sometimes I have the students with red or blond hair share one stanza of the model poem and students with black or brown hair share the next.

On the next poem, I change the directions.

I say, "If you have a summer birthday, stand and read stanza 1. If your birthday is in February, March, or April, you will read stanza 2. For stanza 3, I'd like everyone to stand and share."

Then I ask, "What do you notice about the poems? How are they alike and how do they differ?"

Shelby says that she notices one of the poems is much shorter than the other two.

Ben shares, "Frank Asch has made-up words such as sunball and sundrifts in his 'Sunflakes' poem."

Allie says, "Mr. Harrison's poem is about how sometimes the sun plays tricks on us by going behind the clouds and coming out again." They realize that "sunny" poems can be written in so many ways.

I have written the focus lesson on my trusty easel: "Good writers sometimes web ideas to collect and organize their thoughts." I invite the students to read the focus lesson aloud. Then I ask my students to get out their writers' notebooks and turn to a fresh page.

I say, "Today on this piece of yellow butcher paper that I've taped on the front board, and in your writers' notebooks, we are going to brainstorm and web ideas that have the word *sun* in them or that relate to the sun or to sunny memories that you have." I begin by sharing one or two ideas and then ask them to contribute some ideas. Listening carefully, I begin to fill in the rays of our sun web.

"Tonight I would like you to take your notebooks home and try to add a few more ideas. Remember to bring them back tomorrow, without fail!"

Day Two   *(30-40 minutes or less)*

Webbing Ideas (Be sure it's a sunny day!)

Today we are going to take our notebooks outside and add to our webs. (I take my notebook out, too.) In the front of our school is a lovely flower garden and a small park with benches shaded by aspen trees. I ask my students to find a quiet place and to spend a few minutes savoring the beauty of the day. Then I say, "Now I would like you to add new ideas to your webs. You will have about 15 minutes, so use your time wisely. I'll be writing, too."

After 15 to 20 minutes, we return to our classroom. I ask them to share using quiet voices, in groups of two to four students.

Next I ask, "Does anyone have any new ideas that he or she would like to share with the entire class?" Every hand in the room shoots up! I add their ideas to our class "sun" web. In my room, we learn from one another so the students at this stage of the process are allowed to "steal" ideas. I also invite them to add ideas to our class web as they think of them during the day.

Day Three   *(45-60 minutes or less)*

Drafting the Poems

We begin this day by taking out our sunny poems and reading them aloud. Then I put copies of the poems from page 121 (one poem at a time) on the overhead and once again ask them what they notice. I say, "Today you are going to be poetic sleuths." They mention the different shapes of the poems, the strong verbs, the descriptive words that the poets selected, and the number of stanzas. Using a marker, I jot their observations on each overhead. After we finish discussing the poems, I ask the students to come over to my easel to look over our class sun web, and we work together to compose a sunny poem.

Now it's time for students to return to their desks, carefully study their webs, and circle the ideas that seem to be the most interesting. At this time, I ask them to write the first draft of their poem. I tell them that they have "poetic license" to write whatever type of poem they want. It might rhyme. It might be a list poem. It might be free verse. The object of this lesson is for them to write something that has a personal meaning.

After a few minutes, I ask them to share in small groups. In their groups, each student is invited to jot ideas on the Two Strengths and One Change sheet. When each student has finished sharing, the other members of the group hand

Name _____   Date _____

Two Strengths and One Change

Two specific Strengths

1. _____

2. _____

One Possible Change

1. _____

the sheets to the child. (*The first time that I introduce this strategy, I model it for the class using an overhead.)

Day Four *(45-60 minutes or less)*

Sharing the Poems

It is bright October morning. I ask the class to get out their drafts and carefully reread their poems. They can share with a partner or read them to themselves. At this time I have them revise their drafts, and then I edit with them. The next step is that they either handwrite their final draft or type it up on a computer.

EXTENSION IDEA . . . .

This project could be incorporated into a weather unit or a solar system unit. In this case, I would have the students incorporate some factual information into their poetry.

Student Poems

SUNNY THOUGHTS
by Allie Reava

Mountains so high
that they touch the sky
The grand old flag gracefully
dancing in the wind

Biting into a steamy banana muffin
still hot from the oven
Gazing up at golden
lined clouds
Colors as bright and
cheerful as a rainbow

These are the thoughts that
warm my heart

SUNNY THOUGHTS
by Khalil Arcady

The bristling leaves in a
    strong tall tree
The pointy green grass in
    the big field.
The crystal light rocks in
    my garden
Ms. Kline's soft bunny
    named Cookie
Lovely blooming daffodils
My beautiful mom like
    a soft petaled pink rose
Bathing in a lake of
    of sunflakes
Snow shooting down on a
    winter day
Sunshine on my shoulders
    makes me happy
Red, orange, blue and pink
    birds flying everywhere
A mysterious monarch
    butterfly landing on my nose
Angels flying inside the heavenly
    Gate

Poetry Page

SUNFLAKES
by Frank Asch

If sunlight fell like snowflakes,
gleaming yellow and so bright,
we could build a sunman,
we could have a sunball fight,
we could watch the sunflakes
drifting in the sky.
We could go sleighing
in the middle of July
through sundrifts and sunbanks,
we could ride a sunmobile,
and we could touch sunflakes—
I wonder how they'd feel.

SUN GAMES
by David L. Harrison

The sun is playing
games today,
he touched my face
then slipped away
behind a cloud
where I can't see
and now he's peeking
out at me

As if to promise
in a while
he'll warm me with
his dazzling smile
till like a lizard
on a limb
I'll lazily
look up at him
and blink and nod
without a care,
content to drink
his sun drenched air

And when I finally
get my fill
the sun games
will continue still
until he plays
his last surprise
and slowly, slyly
shuts my eyes.

Using the Power of Poetry to Teach Language Arts, Social Studies, Science, and More *Scholastic Professional Books*

FROM DAVID'S TRAVELS

The Power of Association

Generating Ideas for Writing

> An idea is a feat of association.
>
> –Robert Frost

Practicing the act of association provides more than one benefit. First, it stimulates the imagination to produce numerous ideas in a short period of time. Armed with this process, it's hard for a student to say, "I can't think of anything to write about."

Focus Lesson:

Good writers practice their powers of association
to find ideas for their writing.

• • • • • • •

A writer might be defined as someone who can't stand a blank sheet of paper. Another way of putting it is that writing begins with the first mark on a blank sheet. The point is that writers know they can't put off writing. Even on days when they don't seem to have an idea in their head, they are still expected to produce. No excuses!

So what do you do, if you're supposed to be writing, and nothing is happening? Here's one way writers can get themselves started. Try this with your students to see how many ideas they generate by the simple act of association.

Day One *(60 minutes or less)*

Showing How It Works

Begin with a story about how association can work. I'll tell you one of mine that you are welcome to use. One evening I sat with a pencil in my hand, staring at a blank sheet of paper, without a thought worth recording. To help break the tension, I began doodling on the paper, just making marks. After a time I wrote, "Build a better mousetrap and the world will beat a path to your door." That's an old expression, meaning that success comes from trying harder and doing better than your competition.

The next thing I knew, my mind associated mousetrap with mouse. Mouse made me think of cheese. Cheese made me think of the old saying that

Materials Suggested

- ☙ Board or easel
- ☙ Writers' notebooks
- ☙ Poem: "The Man on the Moon," by David L. Harrison (page 125)
- ☙ Association List Sheet (page 126)

the moon is made of cheese. Moon made me think of the man on the moon. And what, I wondered, would the man on the moon have to eat? You got it: cheese! And so I wrote the poem "The Man on the Moon" on a day when I began with nothing to write about. If you choose to read that poem, ask your students to remember how I let my mind wander from one subject to the next until I found an idea I wanted to write about.

Now you can invite your students to get out their writers' notebooks and start a fresh page, which they will entitle "Associations." Then you can go to the board or easel and write a single word toward the top at the far left. Any word will do. Here is an example using *car*:

"What does *car* make you think about?" you might ask.

"Going fast," someone might say.

"My sister's driving."

"Shiny."

"Noisy."

"Going on vacation."

"My dad bringing me to school."

As the list grows, record each key word or phrase below the starter word, *car*. Keep the associations moving quickly and allow only a brief time for this part of the exercise. The list doesn't need to be long.

Next, take any one word or phrase from the list and begin a new column to the right. For example, you might start the new column with "going on vacation." Then say, "And what does going on vacation make you think about?"

Under the second column, you might record such associations as "Getting packed," "Staying in motels," "Sharing the back seat," "Taking our dog with us," and so on. This is a good time to point out how far we've already come from the single word, "car." But we're not finished. We want one more column.

NOTE: You could keep making columns all day, but three will prove the point of this exercise.

Take something from column two and use it to begin column three. For example, use "sharing the backseat."

"And what does sharing the backseat make you think about?" you might ask.

"Getting licked by our dog."

"Dropping ice cream in my lap."

"Fighting with my brother."

Now you have three lists, which your students can record in their writers' notebooks. You can model how to use association by choosing something from any of the lists and explaining why you like the idea and what you might decide to write about it.

Ask how many students have already spotted something on the lists that they might like to write about. Some may want to share what they have chosen. Give the class until the next day to think about the lists. Tell them that by tomorrow you want everyone to pick a subject they want to write about.

Day Two *(20 minutes or less)*

Drafting Poems

Go around the room, asking each child to announce what he or she has chosen from the association lists to write about. Remind them how easy it was to make lists by associating one idea to the next the way that writers sometimes do it. Pass out copies of the Association List Sheet (page 126) and tell them they can use this to help them make other associations anytime they are stuck for an idea.

NOTE: What kind of poem you ask your students to write is up to you. This exercise is merely a useful tool to help students learn to generate ideas.

EXTENSION IDEA...

You can adapt the associations approach to any unit you are teaching. For example, if you're doing a unit on math, begin by using a key word like "add" or "number" or "math." For science as well, choose words that apply to what your students are studying. That way we reinforce what's going on in class by encouraging students to associate words and phrases with what they're learning. And the poems they write are reinforced by their growing interest in the subject. This is another good way to use poetry as positive reinforcement across the curricula.

Poetry Page

THE MAN ON THE MOON
By David L. Harrison

The man on the moon
Eats nothing but cheese,
There's nothing but cheese to eat,
And often he cries
To the cheddar skies,
"I'd die for just some little treat!"

"I dream of chicken
salad," he sighs,
"On slices of fresh whole wheat,
And I yearn for yams
With sugar-cured hams
And anything gooey and sweet."

But the man on the moon
Has nothing but cheese
So cheese is all he can eat,
But oh how he wishes
For tastier dishes
Like salads and veggies and meat!

Association List Sheet

1. Begin by placing a word or phrase on the top line of Column 1.

2. Below that, list words and phrases you associate with it.

3. Pick something from the list and put it on the top line of Column 2.

4. Below that, make a second list of associations.

5. Pick something from the list and put it on the top line of Column 3.

6. Below that, make a third list of associations.

Column 1	Column 2	Column 3
_____	_____	_____
_____	_____	_____
_____	_____	_____
_____	_____	_____
_____	_____	_____
_____	_____	_____
_____	_____	_____
_____	_____	_____
_____	_____	_____
_____	_____	_____
_____	_____	_____

POETRY BOOKLISTS

~ANTHOLOGIES~

Cullinan, Bernice E. (editor). *A Jar of Tiny Stars: Poems by NCTE Award-Winning Poets*. Boyds Mills Press, 1995.

Goldstein, Bobbye S. *Inner Chimes*. Boyds Mill Press, 1992.

Kennedy, X.J. and Dorothy M. Kennedy. *Talking Like the Rain: A Read-to-Me Book of Poems*. Little, Brown, 1992.

Koch, Kenneth and Kate Farrell. *Talking to the Sun: An Illustrated Anthology of Poems for Young People*. Metropolitan Museum of Art/Henry Holt, 1985.

Moore, Lilian. *Sunflakes*. Clarion, 1992.

Prelutsky, Jack. *The Random House Book of Poetry for Children*. Random House, 1983.

Rosen, Michael. *Classic Poetry: An Illustrated Collection*. Candlewick, 1998.

Strickland, Michael R. *My Own Song*. Boyds Mills Press, 1997.

Strickland, Michael R. *Poems That Sing to You*. Boyds Mills Press, 1993.

Whipple, Laura. *Celebrating America*. Philomel, 1994.

Yolen, Jane. *Once Upon Ice and Other Frozen Poems*. Boyds Mills Press, 1997.

Yolen, Jane. *Sing Noel*. Boyds Mills Press, 1996.

Yolen, Jane. *Sleep Rhymes Around the World*. Boyds Mills Press, 1994.

Yolen, Jane. *Street Rhymes Around the World*. Boyds Mills Press, 1992.

~EMOTIONS, FAMILY, PETS, FRIENDS, AND FEELINGS~

Ciardi, John. *The Monster Den*. Boyds Mills Press, 1991.

Ciardi, John. *You Know Who*. Boyds Mills Press, 1991.

Fletcher, Ralph. *Relatively Speaking*. Orchard, 1999.

Greenfield, Eloise. *Honey, I Love*. Harper Trophy, 1986.

Harrison, David. *A Thousand Cousins*. Boyds Mills Press, 1995.

Holbrook, Sara. *Am I Naturally This Crazy?* Boyds Mills Press, 1997.

Holbrook, Sara. *I Never Said I Wasn't Difficult*. Boyds Mills Press, 1997.

Holbrook, Sara. *Walking on the Boundaries of Change*. Boyds Mills Press, 1998.

Holbrook, Sara. *Which Way to the Dragon!* Boyds Mills Press, 1997.

Hopkins, Lee Bennett. *Been to Yesterdays*. Boyds Mills Press, 1999.

Hughes, Langston. *The Dream Keeper and Other Poems*. Alfred A. Knopf, 1986.

Johnston, Tony. *It's About Dogs*. Harcourt, Inc., 2000.

Micklos, John, Jr. (compiler). *Daddy Poems*. Boyds Mills Press, 2000.

Micklos, John, Jr. (compiler). *Mommy Poems*. Boyds Mills Press, 2001.

Yolen, Jane. *Dear Mother, Dear Daughter*. Boyds Mills Press, 2001.

~POEMS FOR MONTHS AND SEASONS OF THE YEAR~

Baird, Audrey B. *Storm Coming!* Boyds Mills Press, 2001.

Booth, David. *Voices on the Wind*. Morrow Junior Books, 1990.

Dotlich, Rebecca Kai. *Lemonade Sun*. Boyds Mills Press, 1998.

Florian, Douglas. *Winter Eyes*. Greenwillow, 1999.

Frank, Josette. *Snow Toward Evening*. Dial, 1990.

Smith, William Jay and Carol Ra. *The Sun Is Up: A Child's Year of Poems*. Boyds Mills Press, 1996.

Winnick, Karen B. *A Year Goes Round: Poems for the Months*. Boyds Mills Press, 2001.

Yolen, Jane. *Snow, Snow: Winter Poems for Children*. Boyds Mills Press, 1998.

~SCHOOL POETRY~

Bagert, Brod. *Chicken Socks*. Boyds Mills Press, 1994.

Dakos, Kalli. *If You're Not Here, Please Raise Your Hand*. Aladdin, 1995.

Harrison, David. *Somebody Catch My Homework*. Boyds Mills Press, 1993.

Holbrook, Sara. *The Dog Ate My Homework*. Boyds Mills Press, 1997.

Sheilds, Carol Diggory. *Lunch Money and Other Poems About School*. Dutton, 1995.

~GENERAL AND HUMOROUS~

Bagert, Brod. *Let Me Be the Boss . . . .* Boyds Mills Press, 1992.

Carroll, Lewis. *The Walrus and the Carpenter*. Boyds Mills Press, 1998.

Ciardi, John. *Someone Could Win a Polar Bear*. Boyds Mills Press, 2002.

Dotlich, Rebecca Kai. *When Riddles Come Rumbling*. Boyds Mills Press, 2001.

Harley, Avis. *Fly With Poetry*. Boyds Mills Press, 2000.

Harley, Avis. *Leap Into Poetry: More ABCs of Poetry*. Boyds Mills Press, 2001.

Harrison, David. *The Boy Who Counted Stars*. Boyds Mills Press, 1994.

Harrison, David. *Farmer's Garden: Rhymes for Two Voices*. Boyds Mills Press, 2000.

Spinelli, Eileen. *Tea Party Today*. Boyds Mills Press, 1998.

Terban, Marvin. *Time to Rhyme: A Rhyming Dictionary*. Boyds Mills Press, 1994.

~MATH~

Hopkins, Lee Bennett. *It's About Time!* Simon and Schuster, 1993.

Hopkins, Lee Bennett. *Marvelous Math.* Simon and Schuster, l997.

~READING, LANGUAGE ARTS, AND PLAYING WITH WORDS~

Bennett, Jill. *Noisy Poems.* Oxford University Press, 1987.

Bennett, Jill. *A Packet of Poems.* Oxford University Press, l989.

Bennett, Jill. *Tasty Poems.* Oxford University Press, l992.

Fleischman, Paul. *Joyful Noise: Poems for Two Voices.* Harper and Row, l988.

Hopkins, Lee Bennett. *Good Books, Good Times!* HarperCollins, l990.

Worth, Valerie. *All the Small Poems.* Sunburst, 1991.

~SCIENCE, ECOLOGY, NATURE, AND OBSERVATION~

Daniel, Mark. *A Child's Treasury of Seaside Verse.* Dial, 1991.

Dotlich, Rebecca Kai. *Sweet Dreams of the Wild: Poems for Bedtime.* Boyds Mills Press, 1996.

Fletcher, Ralph. *Ordinary Things.* Atheneum, 1997.

Harrison, David. *The Purchase of Small Secrets.* Boyds Mills Press, 1998.

Harrison, David. *Wild Country.* Boyds Mills Press, 1999.

Heard, Georgia. *Creatures of Earth, Sea, and Sky.* Boyds Mills Press, 1992.

Yolen, Jane. *Color Me A Rhyme.* Boyds Mills Press, 2000.

Yolen, Jane (selector). *Mother Earth Father Sky: Poems of Our Planet.* Boyds Mills Press, 1996.

Yolen, Jane. *Water Music.* Boyds Mills Press, 1995.

~SOCIAL STUDIES~

Bishop, Rudine Sims (editor). *Wonders: The Best Children's Poems of Effie Lee Newsome.* Boyds Mills Press, 2000.

De Fina, Allan A. *When a City Leans Against the Sky.* Boyds Mills Press, 1997.

Gunning, Monica. *Not a Copper Penny in Me House: Poems From the Caribbean.* Boyds Mills Press, 1993.

Gunning, Monica. *Under the Breadfruit Tree: Island Poems.* Boyds Mills Press, 1998.

Hopkins, Lee Bennett. *My America: A Poetry Atlas of the United States.* Simon and Schuster, 2000.

Medina, Jane. *My Name is Jorge.* Boyds Mills Press, 1999.

Olaleye, Isaac. *The Distant Talking Drum: Poems from Nigeria.* Boyds Mills Press, 1995.

Strickland, Dorothy S. and Michael R. Strickland (editors), *Families: Poems Celebrating the African American Experience.* Boyds Mills Press, 1994.

Weatherford, Carole Boston, *Sidewalk Chalk: Poems of the City.* Boyds Mills Press, 2001.

Yolen, Jane. *Sky Scrape/City Scape: Poems of City Life.* Boyds Mills Press, 1996.

~SPORTS AND ACTIVITIES~

Hopkins, Lee Bennett. *Opening Days.* Harcourt, Brace and Company, 1996.

Janeczko, Paul B. *That Sweet Diamond: Baseball Poems.* Athenuem, l998.

Liatsos, Sandra Olson. *Bicycle Riding and Other Poems.* Boyds Mills Press, 1997.

Morrison, Lillian. *Way to Go!* Boyds Mills Press, 2001.

~TEACHER RESOURCES~

Benton, Michael, J. Teasey, R. Bell, E.K. Hurst. *Young Readers Responding to Poems.* Routledge, 1988.

Chatton, Barbara. *Using Poetry Across the Curriculum.* Oryx, 1993.

Cullinan, Bernice E., Marilyn Scala, Virginia Schroder. *Three Voices: An Invitation to Poetry Across the Curriculum.* Teachers Pub Group, 1995.

Denman, Gregory. *When You've Made It Your Own.* Heinemann, 1988.

Graham, Paula W. *Speaking of Journals.* Boyds Mills Press, 1999.

Graves, Donald. *Explore Poetry.* Heinemann, 1992.

Harrison, David and Bernice E. Cullinan. *Easy Poetry Lessons That Dazzle and Delight.* Scholastic, 1999.

Heard, Georgia. *For the Good of the Earth and Sun.* Heinemann, 1989.

Hulme, Joy N. and Donna W. Guthrie. *How to Write, Recite, and Delight in All Kinds of Poetry.* Millbrook, 1996.

Janeczko, Paul B. *Favorite Poetry Lessons.* Scholastic Professional Books, 1998.

Janeczko, Paul B. *The Place My Words Are Looking For.* Bradbury Press, 1990.

Larrick, Nancy. *Let's Do a Poem!* Delacorte, 1991.

Livingston, Myra Cohn. *Poem-Making: Ways to Begin Writing Poetry.* HarperCollins, 1991.

Routman, Regie. *Kids' Poems.* Scholastic Professional Books, 2000.

Steinbergh, Judith. *Reading and Writing Poetry.* Scholastic Professional Books, 1994.

Sweeney, Jacqueline. *Quick Poetry Activities.* Scholastic Professional Books, 1994.

Sweeney, Jacqueline. *Teaching Poetry: Yes You Can!* Scholastic Professional Books, 1993.